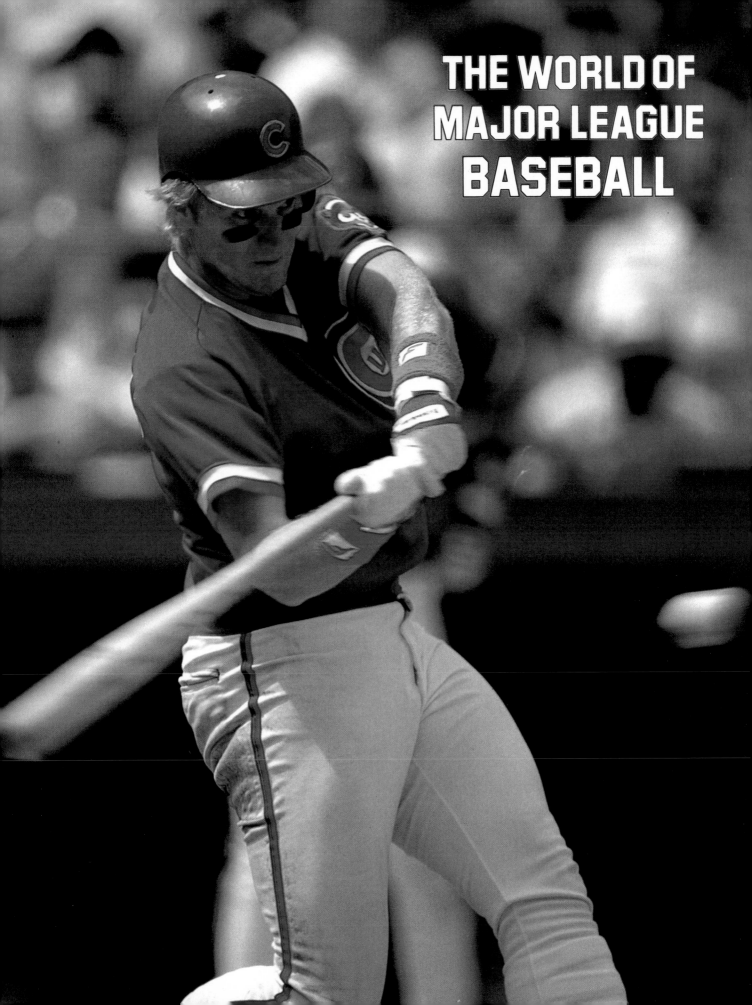

THE WORLD OF MAJOR LEAGUE BASEBALL

CLB 1789
©1987 Colour Library Books Ltd.,
   Guildford, Surrey, England.
© 1987 Illustrations: Chuck Solomon,
   New York, U.S.A.
Designed by Philip Clucas.
Printed and bound in Barcelona, Spain
   by Cronion, S.A.
All rights reserved.
1987 edition published by Crescent Books,
   distributed by Crown Publishers, Inc.
ISBN 0 517 62924 0
h g f e d c b a

Photographer's Dedication
This book is dedicated with love
   to Ellen and Lauren.

Author's Dedication
To Lewis; more than a good
   brother, a good friend.

THE WORLD OF
MAJOR LEAGUE
BASEBALL

Photography by   Text by
Chuck Solomon   Paul Fichtenbaum

CRESCENT BOOKS~NEW YORK

CONTENTS

FOREWORD

by Chuck Solomon

Welcome to the world of Major League Baseball. In this volume I've tried to capture in pictures the excitement of America's national pastime.

Photographing baseball presents some unique challenges. The photographer must constantly ask himself questions if he is to anticipate the players' actions and the managers' strategies. Will Coleman run on the next pitch? Will Brett try to hit to the opposite field? Will Parrish call for a pitch out? And then, he has to be in position photographically in order to be focused where the action is most likely to occur.

By contrast, he must also be aware of the quiet moments in baseball: the look of dejection after a player has struck out; the manager's thoughtfulness when deciding whether or not to remove a pitcher. Since baseball is a game not only of spontaneous action but also of studied contemplation, a balanced photographic record requires the man behind the camera to capture both characteristics.

For this he needs to be fully prepared technically, having the right lens ready for any given situation — a long telephoto to shoot tight and capture the emotion on a player's face; a shorter lens to show several players involved in an important play; perhaps a wide-angle to photograph the surroundings of the ballpark. And, of course, film choice is equally important: one usually tries to stick to slow, fine-grain film in daylight, and faster, high-speed film when shooting night games.

So it's not just a question of sitting in your photo position taking pictures at leisure. Photography is hard and fast work if the pictures are to reflect the game's drama and excitement.

And no matter what excites *you* about the game of baseball — whether it be Schmidt hitting a home run, Clemens striking out a batter, or Barfield throwing out a runner at the plate — I hope that you'll find that the images in this book, and of course the informative text which surrounds them, help you capture some of the special sights and sounds of baseball at its best and its stars at their most brilliant.

THE WORLD SERIES

The 1986 World Series might be best remembered as The One That Slipped Away. Or maybe even, The One That Slipped Through. But whatever you want to call it, The New York Mets were the big winners, the Boston Red Sox the big losers.

Who could ever forget the scene of the Boston dugout in the 10th inning of Game Six? The Sox led, 5-3, on a home run by Dave Henderson and an RBI single by Marty Barrett. There was starter Roger Clemens, fingers crossed, three outs away from Boston's first World Championship since 1918. Perched on the top step were Jim Rice and Don Baylor, the two elder statesmen. Boston forgot to bring the champagne, so the Mets, now expecting to cry in their beer, not celebrate with bubbly, courteously transferred the champagne to the Boston clubhouse.

Reliever Calvin Schiraldi, the ace of the Boston bullpen who came to the Red Sox in a winter deal with the Mets, got Wally Backman to fly out Keith Hernandez to line out and was one strike away from ending it with Ray Knight. So disconsolate was Hernandez that he left the field and went into manager Davey Johnson's office to watch the game on television.

Then the nightmare started for Schiraldi and the Red Sox. Gary Carter singled. Kevin Mitchell pinch-hit a single. Then Ray Knight with two strikes, cracked one up the middle to drive in Carter, and the Mets miraculously pulled within one run, 5-4, with Mitchell on third. At that point, Hernandez made his way from the clubhouse back to the dugout. Quickly he recanted, scooting back to Johnson's office saying, "There were a lot of hits left in that chair."

Boston skipper John McNamara had enough of Schiraldi and brought in Bob Stanley to face Mookie Wilson. Stanley was not exactly a favorite with Red Sox fans, who booed his every move in the regular season. But Stanley was unaffected by the fans' booing, saying only, "That's OK. When I'm on the mound in the World Series, they'll cheer me."

There he was, ready to be cheered and all he had to do was get the final out and Boston would wear a championship ring. "It's the dream of every major league pitcher," said Stanley, "to be on the mound for the world champions."

Stanley and Wilson fought the count to 2 and 2, with Wilson fouling off two tough breaking balls to stay alive. Now that Wilson was chomping at the breaking ball, Stanley decided to throw an inside fastball. And he did. Too inside. Wilson jumped out of the way, catcher Rich Gedman lunged with his glove only to have it hit the edge and travel to the screen. Mitchell hesitated, then made a mad dash to the plate. "i didn't know if I was going to make it," he said later. "Four steps from the plate I was going to dive. Then I saw I didn't have to." The only thing Mitchell and the Mets saw was the score tied at 5-5.

But the drama was far from over. Knight moved to second base on the

The Mets parachuted (above) into the World Series against the Red Sox and both teams had reason to celebrate (facing page). Gary Carter slaps a tag on Jim Rice as Dave Henderson looks on (overleaf, main) while Bruce Hurst (inset) starred on the hill.

wild pitch and the Red Sox bench took one giant step back, the disappointment topped only by shock. The count was now 3 and 2 on Wilson. He fouled off the next pitch. Then he hit a weak grounder to first baseman Bill Buckner, who hobbled all series with a severe leg problem.

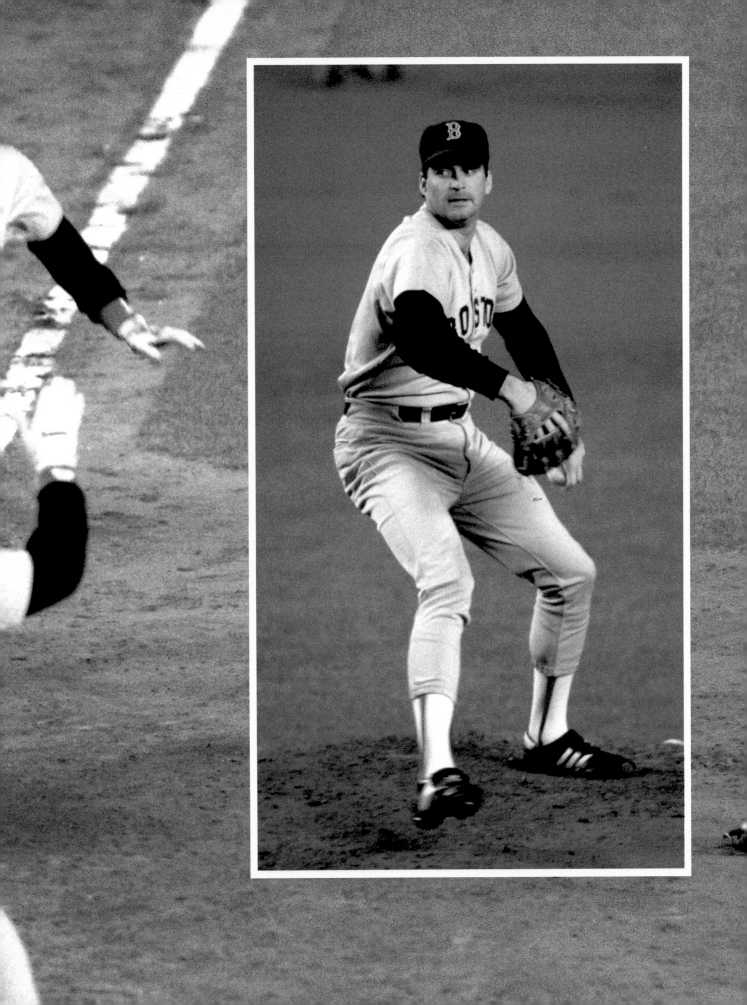

his counterpart Roger Clemens taking the hill for Boston, Game Two figured to be a fabulous duel between baseball's top two pitchers. What it turned out to be was the poorest game of the series, the Red Sox crushing the Mets 9-3 behind an 18-hit attack. Gooden lasted only five innings, yielding six runs and eight hits. Clemens wasn't a world-beater either, as he departed before five innings and didn't even earn the win.

The series moved to Fenway Park for Games Three, Four and, hopefully for the Mets, Game Five. Before any pitch was thrown at Fenway, manager Davey Johnson provided the Mets with a big boost. Instead of working out on Monday, Johnson gave his tired troops the day off. After a physically and mentally draining series against Houston, the Mets were flat against the Sox in the first two games. Knowing his players as he does, Johnson opted for the day off and the Mets responded in a big way.

Their bats had been slow all post-season, but the Mets started off right when Len Dykstra belted a lead-off homer off Oil Can Boyd to give the New Yorkers a lift. Bob Ojeda, who was the Mets main man in the Calvin Schiraldi deal, pitched a gutty game, allowing five hits in a 7-1 victory and getting the Mets back into the series. Following the game, he said he didn't really have any bad feelings toward his old team, although several took shots at him.

"See this jacket," said Ojeda, wearing a Mets logo on the chest. "The last thing I feel is bittersweetness. It's competition out there. Everybody wants to knock everybody else's socks off."

In Game Five, Boston skipper John McNamara took a gamble by starting Al Nipper. His earned run average of 5.38 was the highest for a series starter since Hal Gregg's 5.87 for the Dodgers in 1947. Despite his bloated e.r.a., Nipper performed well, allowing only three runs in six innings.

But this was an easy one. All Buckner had to do was field the ball and flip it to Stanley covering the bag. Easy, right?

Well, "it bounced and bounced and then it didn't bounce," said Buckner. "It skipped." And while the ball skipped through his legs, Ray Knight skipped home with the winning run, the Mets skipped right back into the series and denied the Red Sox the chance to skip home with the silverware.

After the game the Red Sox did catch a break. Weather reports forecast rain for Game Seven and if the Sox could get an extra day off, they could pitch Bruce Hurst, the Mets' nemesis so far in the series. In Game One, Hurst shut out the Mets, 1-0, at Shea Stadium. The 28-year-old southpaw dazzled the New Yorkers with his looping overhand curve and forkball. He allowed only four hits over eight innings and outpitched Ron Darling, who was equally effective, yielding only an unearned run in the seventh inning on an error by second baseman Tim Teufel.

Game Four provided the same result for the Sox and Hurst. This time he scattered 10 hits as the Sox won 4-2 in Fenway Park. Like Houston's Mike Scott in the playoffs, it was apparent that Hurst had the Mets number.

After dropping the first game, everybody expected the Mets to come back strong, especially having Dwight Gooden on the mound. With

Former Red Sox hurler Bob Ojeda (above left) came back to haunt his old team by winning Game Three in Boston for the Mets. Boston catcher Rich Gedman had a busy series at home plate, here tagging Gary Carter (facing page top) and then combining with Wade Boggs to run-down Mookie Wilson (facing page bottom).

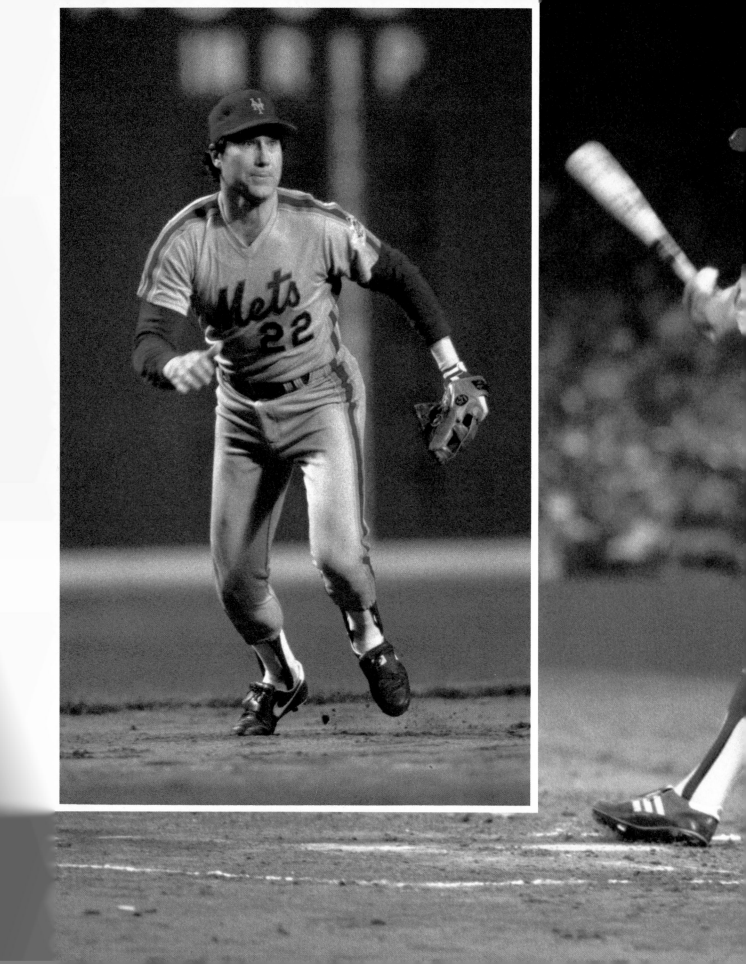

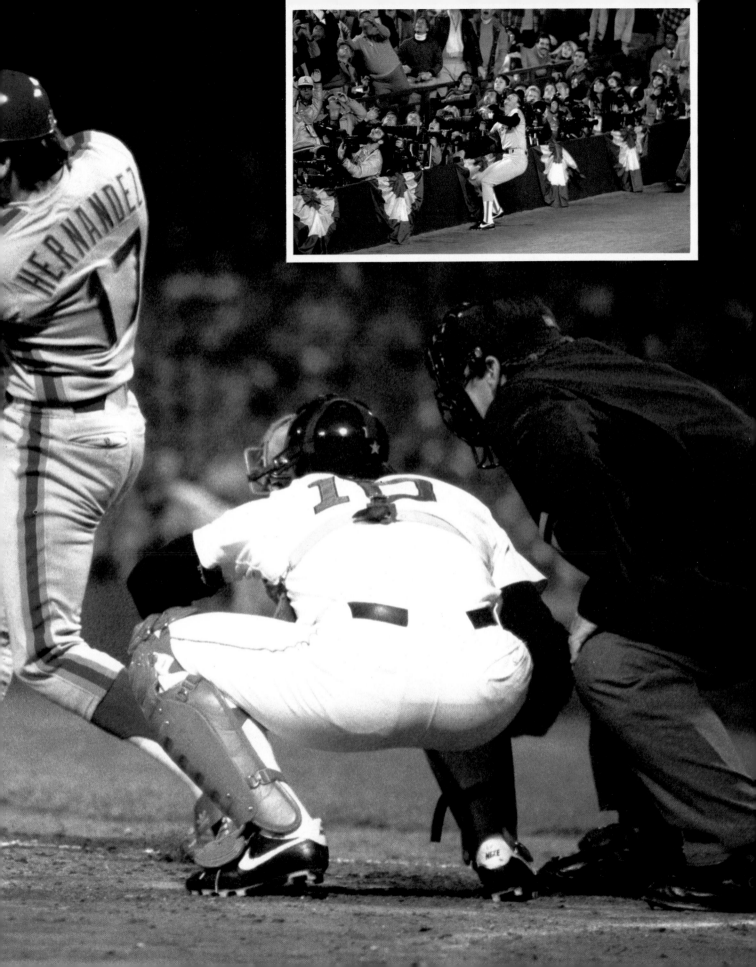

starters and into the bullpen, they would win. "I wouldn't have said this during the Series," said Mets second baseman Wally Backman, "but we knew that if we got to the bullpen, it would be no contest.

And, as it turned out, it wasn't. Schiraldi replaced Hurst to start the seventh frame. Knight worked the count to 2-1 and readied himself for one of Schiraldi's 95 mile-per-hour fastballs. And he got it, sending it deep into the left field bleachers to give the Mets a 4-3 lead.

"I decided to be real aggressive," Knight said after winning the World Series MVP. "I looked in a zone and he threw it there. It was probably my greatest thrill in baseball."

The Mets tacked on two more runs for insurance, and as it turned out they needed it. With the score 6-3, Boston erupted for two runs off Mets reliever Roger McDowell. With the tying run on second and no outs, Davey Johnson brought in lefthander Jessie Orosco

It didn't matter though, as Ron Darling continued to sparkle in the post-season, this time pitching the Mets to a 6-2 victory featuring two home runs over the Green Monster by Gary Carter.

After the shock of losing Game Six, The One That Slipped Away, the weather cooperated, giving Boston an edge. A day-long downpour forced commissioner Peter Ueberroth to postpone the game until Monday, allowing Boston to pitch Hurst on three days' rest and also giving them an extra day to forget the disaster that was Game Six.

It looked like the man upstairs was finally with the Sox as Hurst breezed along with a 3-0 lead in the finale. Boston jumped all over Darling in the second inning, scoring three runs,

including solo homers by Rich Gedman and Dwight Evans. As NBC's Vin Scully said, "It's so quiet in New York, you can almost hear them cheering in Boston."

But the cheering stopped in the bottom of the sixth. Lee Mazzilli came off the Mets' bench to deliver a pinch hit single. Wilson added another single and a walk to Teufel loaded the bases for Hernandez. The man they call Mex came through in a big way, smacking an eye-high pitch to centerfield to score two runs. Carter followed that with a single to right and the score was knotted at three. Boston fans could no longer be heard, even if they all congregated in the Shea Stadium parking lot.

All series, the Mets quietly felt that if they could get by the Boston

Keith Hernandez and Series MVP Ray Knight (previous page main and left inset) led the Mets while Wade Boggs (inset right) sparkled in the field. Hernandez holds Boggs on (above left) and Gedman (above) chases a foul then collides with Carter and Dykstra (facing page top and bottom).

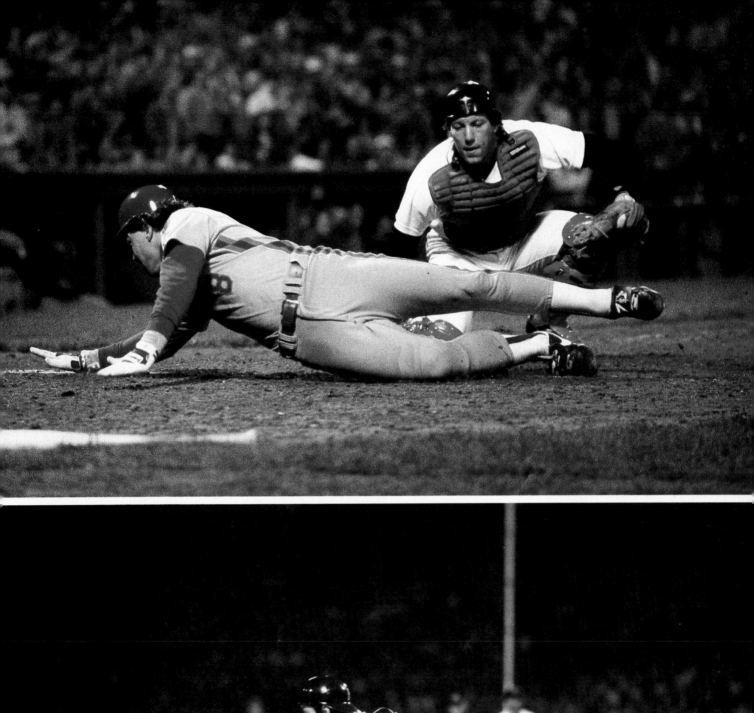

Dwight Evans (main picture) cracked a home run off Ron Darling in Game Six. Jessie Orosco (inset top) saved Game Seven for the Mets and manager Davey Johnson (inset bottom).

to put out the fire. Orosco got Gedman on a liner to second, Henderson on strikes, then induced Don Baylor to ground out to shortstop Rafael Santana. New York put the finishing touches on the game when Darryl Strawberry hit a towering home run to right and Orosco singled in another run.

And when Orosco struck out Marty Barrett to end the game and the World Series, the Mets were finally crowned World Champions.

"We deserve it," said Davey Johnson. "We had the best record in baseball. We should be the champions. Boston is a great team, but the good guys got it. This is what we all sweated for."

"To be traded here, to a last-place team, to see them turn it around in three years...," said an exhausted

Ray Knight and wife Nancy (above) enjoy the parade while Gary Carter (left) salutes the crowd. New York stopped for a day to celebrate (facing page).

Hernandez. "I played when there were 2,000 people at Shea. Now the fans are all back. It's the greatest feeling in the world for me."

In the years to come, many probably won't remember exactly how the Mets won the championship in Game Seven. What they'll remember about the 1986 Fall Classic is Game Six – The One That Slipped Through.

"I can't remember the last time I missed a ground ball," said Buckner, the goat of the Series. "I'll remember that one."

So will the rest of the Red Sox.

★ THE ★
PLAYOFFS

When Casey Stengel nicknamed the New York Mets Amazin', there must have been some divine reason for it. For how else could anyone explain the incredible six-game series between the Houston Astros and the Mets to determine the National League Champion and World Series participant?

Sure the Mets prevailed four games to two, but it's the way they did it that was so, uh, amazin'. Consider that, not counting the second game, the New Yorkers led in the series only four innings in the 58 played. Consider that the Mets' batters, who led the league in hitting during the regular season, set new records for futility in both average and strikeouts. Consider that Dwight Gooden, the Mets' number one pitcher, didn't win one game and Mike Scott, the eventual Cy Young Award winner for the Astros, hurled 18 innings and allowed only one run.

And then consider the Mets' heroes. Before the series began, who could have imagined that 5-9, 175 pound Len Dykstra would be the power source? Or Jesse Orosco, who lost his stopper role out of the bullpen to Roger McDowell in the regular campaign, would come on and win three games for the Mets in relief?

But the unexpected is the way it had been for New York all season. New heroes every night for the winners of 108 games, a team that all but wrapped up its division by July 4, the Mets were a team of characters and character. It was that character which dealt Houston agonizing blows all series.

Think back to Game Three, the series tied at one game each and Houston leading 4-0 heading into the bottom of the sixth. The Mets knot the score on Darryl Strawberry's home run and win the game with two-run homer from Dykstra in the bottom of the ninth. Then think back to Game Five, the series again tied, and the game in extra innings. The bottom of the 12th brings up Gary Carter, mired in a horrendous 1-21 slump, and who promptly singles in the winning run.

But the game Houston doesn't want to think back to at all was Game Six, the series finale.

At that point everything was going in Houston's favor. Sure the Mets led the series 3-2, but Bob Knepper had the Mets in a hole, trailing 3-0 in the

The Astros' Mike Scott (above) dominated the Mets throughout the League Championship Series, winning both times he faced New York. Glenn Davis (facing page top) won Game One with a homer. Rafael Santana slaps a tag on Billy Hatcher who was attempting to steal second (facing page bottom).

ninth inning. With the specter of Mike Scott looming huge in the dugout waiting to pitch the seventh game, the Astros were feeling good. After all, Scott handled the Mets easily so far, so easily that they accused him of scuffing the baseballs with sandpaper. Not only was Scott making quick work of the Mets hitters in the batter's box, but he also had them psyched out before they left the dugout.

Back to the clincher. Heading into the ninth inning, Knepper was in complete control, mowing down 14 straight at one point and keeping the Mets sluggers off stride, mixing an assortment of breaking balls with an occasional fastball. Things fell apart, however, when Dykstra led off with a triple to the centerfield wall. Mookie Wilson singled in Dykstra and Keith Hernandez came through with a clutch double to score Wilson and put himself in position to tie the score. Dave Smith, who blew Game Three when he allowed Dykstra's two-run game-winning homer, entered the game in relief of Knepper. He immediately walked both Carter and Strawberry on 3-2 counts and then

Ray Knight hit a sacrifice fly to send the game into overtime.

Experts who rated the series felt the Mets biggest edge over Houston was in the bullpen, and that point was proven throughout the six games. Roger McDowell relieved for the Mets and pitched five perfect innings. He should have gotten the win in the 14th when the Mets scratched out a run against reliever Aurelio Lopez. But in the bottom of the inning Billy Hatcher hit a Jessie Orosco fastball high on the left-field foul pole screen to knot the game and the stomach of Mets manager Davey Johnson.

But the Mets managed to quell the rumbling in Johnson's midsection by tallying three times in the 16th for what should have been an easy win. Orosco courted disaster in the bottom half, though. After striking out Craig Reynolds he issued a free pass to Davey Lopes, and singles to Bill Doran, Billy Hatcher and Glenn Davis. In between, he forced Denny Walling into a fielder's choice, so now it was down to Orosco vs. Kevin Bass.

Before Bass stepped into the box, Hernandez and Carter went to the mound to discuss tactics. It was then that Hernandez laid down the law. No more fastballs.

"Kid, if you call one more fastball, we're going to fight," Hernandez told Carter, referring to the Mets' backstop by his nickname. Carter called six straight sliders, Bass struck out and the Mets were National League Champions.

"I feel like I've been pardoned," said Davey Johnson following the roller-coaster win.

"We're not unlike a lot of the great teams," said Mets general manager Frank Cashen. "We have this quiet air about us that says, 'We think we are good.' The old Orioles had it. The Dodgers had it. The Reds had it. But because we are from New York, it's interpreted as arrogance."

The Mets seemed less arrogant and more like crybabies after Game One of the series, when Scott overpowered them with his split-fingered fastball. He struck out 14, allowed five hits and outpitched Dwight Gooden, who yielded a second-inning solo homer to Glenn Davis as the Mets fell 1-0.

"His fastball is not really overpowering," said New York second baseman Wally Backman of Scott, "but

when you're looking for the split-finger and he throws the fastball, it *is* overpowering."

The Mets could have taken their post-game speeches from Game One and applied them equally to Game Five. Again Scott was brilliant, this time working on three days rest. Even though he only struck out five, Scott yielded only three hits as the Astros took Game Four 3-1 on a two-run homer by Alan Ashby and a solo shot by Dickie Thon.

In between and after Scott's starts, however, is where the Mets capitalized on their heroics. Game Two was a solid pitching performance by the Mets' best hurler in the regular season, Bob Ojeda. The former Red Sox' southpaw kept the Astros at bay with his changeup while the Mets exploded against Houston's Nolan Ryan. Ryan struck out five of the first six batters he faced, but in the fourth

Tim Teufel avoids a sliding Jose Cruz (above) while Gary Carter singles in the winning run off reliever Charlie Kerfeld in Game Five (right).

inning the Mets touched Ryan for three runs on singles by Backman and Hernandez, a double by Carter and a sacrifice fly by Strawberry. That's all Ojeda needed as the Mets cruised to a 4-1 victory to knot the series.

Games Three, Five and Six, the other Mets victories, bordered on the ridiculous, as the New Yorkers constantly fought from behind to break the hearts of the Houston Astros. If Casey were here, he'd only have one thing to say.

Amazin'!

★★★

Gene Mauch has been through some bad times in his 25 years as a major league manager. He was at the helm for the now infamous Philadelphia Phillies collapse of 1964. He guided the California Angels to a 2-0 advantage over the Milwaukee Brewers in the 1982 playoffs only to see his club lose three straight and the American League pennant. He has never won a pennant as a skipper and only Connie Mack, John McGraw and Bucky Harris have ever managed longer in baseball history. But when it comes to disappointments, the 1986 league championship series loss to the Boston Red Sox was the defeat that probably hurt the most.

The Angels held a commanding three games to one advantage, but eventually blew the pennant in an 8-1 loss at Boston. "I hurt like hell – for the players," said Mauch after the Angels were eliminated and that 25-year monkey on his back gained a few pounds. "They laid their hearts out

there and they got them stepped on. A lot of people have tried to get into my head. If they did get there, though, they wouldn't know what they were dealing with."

What the Angels were dealing with in the final two games of the series was a sinking feeling. After all, you could say that they really lost the series in Game Five. Leading 5-2 and heading into the ninth inning, all the Angels needed was three outs and they were World Series bound. They were two out with a man on base when Don Baylor hit a two-run homer to left field off Mike Witt to bring the Sox within one at 5-4. No sweat, though. The Angels were still in control and Mauch quickly brought in reliever Gary Lucas to pitch to Rich Gedman. The first pitch drilled him in the ribs and the California fans swallowed hard at their fate.

That was the first time in 322 innings, dating back to May 3, 1982, that Lucas plucked a batter. "I don't

Mookie Wilson (previous page main and inset) slides into third baseman Phil Garner ...safely. Donnie Moore and Dave Henderson (above left and right) were the goats and heroes of the AL LCS. Marty Barrett (facing page bottom) is congratulated as Roger Clemens (facing page top) tips his cap to the fans.

know how many years I've got left, but I'd gladly give up the last two of them if I could get that pitch back," said Mauch.

After Lucas' pitch, Mauch summoned his ace righthander, Donnie Moore, out of the bullpen to face Boston righthanded hitter Dave Henderson. With the count 2 and 2 and the police ready to keep the fans from celebrating on the field, Henderson fouled off two consecutive pitches. It was just a matter of time for the Angels and their fans. But as fate would have it,

Henderson hit a split-fingered fastball over the leftfield fence on the next pitch and the Red Sox, amazingly, were leading 6-5. That didn't turn out to be the game-winning hit as California tied the contest in the last of the ninth and the Sox won it in the 11th. But to all intents and purposes, it cost the Angels the game and a berth in the World Series.

"I've already begun thinking about it," Henderson said of the magnitude of his home run. "A lot of years down the road people are going to be replaying it over and over. It was a big home run. I don't know how big the word big means, but it was a big home run."

"That was our Game Seven," said second baseman Marty Barrett, who copped the ALCS Most Valuable Player honors with a record 11 hits. "It took a lot out of them. I think they were in the dugout getting all ready for a celebration. The guards were ready. I heard the ballboys were popping champagne in the clubhouse. They had it. It was theirs. It was dangling out in front of them.

"That was our motivation right there. After that, we were on the gravy train. We were playing with the

house's money. We were playing loose. They knew they should have had it."

Don Baylor, who played on the '82 Angels who blew a 2-0 series lead to Milwaukee, was equally excited.

"I think it was the sweetest win I've ever been involved in. When you're that close to winning and then have that happen. I'll replay that in my mind over and over."

Perhaps that is what the Angels were doing when the series shifted to Boston for the remaining two games. They never seemed to recover from the shock of losing Game Five. In Game Six, the Red Sox offense exploded, giving Oil Can Boyd a 16-hit attack to work with as Boston tied the series.

"All right," said Mauch before Game Seven. "To this point, both teams have shown that they know how to play and that they know how to win. Now we'll try to find out which team knows how to win when it has to win."

It was Boston, hands down. At least, that's how the California fielders played, as errors by shortstop Dick Schofield and center fielder Gary Pettis allowed the Red Sox to score seven unearned runs off losing pitcher John Candelaria. The ironic part of the poor fielding is that Schofield and Pettis committed the errors. Schofield is one of the finer fielding shortstops in the majors, committing just 18 errors all season. And Pettis won the Gold Glove in the American League in 1985. The final score: 8-1.

The Red Sox win marked only the sixth time in 36 post-season situations that a team had rallied from a 3-1 deficit.

"We've been coming from behind all year," said a jubilant Baylor in the Red Sox clubhouse. "Before Sunday in Anaheim (Game Five), a lot of people were thinking the Red Sox always choke, they go down to the wire but never finish it off. But the guys in this clubhouse knew whatever happened in 1978 and other years had nothing to do with the character of this ballclub."

The victory may have made the Boston players and fans forget a lot of disappointment from the past. But for Gene Mauch this may have been the biggest disappointment of his long career.

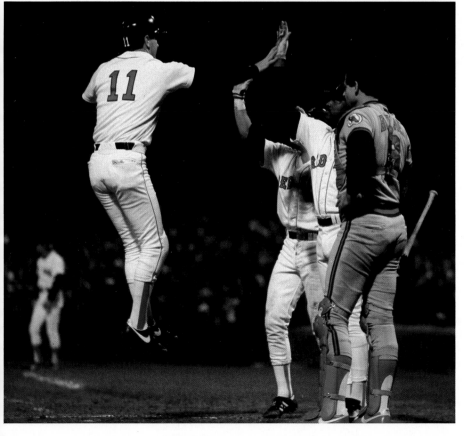

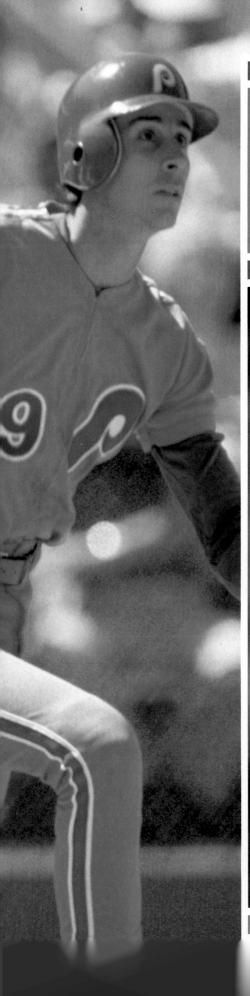

THE LEADERS

The 1986 baseball season was the antithesis of the previous one as far as pennant races were concerned. In 1985, three of the four division titles weren't decided until the final two weeks of the season. The Mets battled the Cardinals, the Yankees tussled with the Blue Jays, and the Royals, the eventual World Champions, fought off the Angels.

But in 1986, the divisional races took shape early and stayed that way through the season. The New York Mets, expected to make a big run at the Cardinals, were leading the National League East by over 20 games in July and coasted home for an easy win. The Houston Astros surprised almost all baseball experts by pulling away from Cincinnati and surprising San Francisco after the All-Star break to win the West by 10 games.

The American League races were tighter, but for most of the season, they were never in doubt. The Red Sox opened a large lead early on the

Mike Schmidt (facing page) won his third N.L. MVP hitting 37 home runs. Dave parker (right) finished second in HRs and RBI while Rickey Henderson (below) took the A.L. stolen base crown.

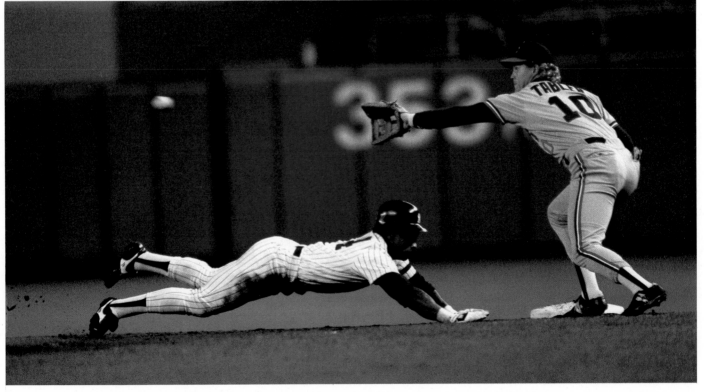

Keith Hernandez (left) finished fifth in the N.L. with a .310 average. Jessie Barfeld of the Blue Jays (right) led the majors in home runs with 40.

incredible pitching exploits of Roger Clemens and held off the Yankees to win their first division title since 1975. The California Angels, thought to be too old to mount a challenge in the West, rode their excellent pitching staff to a victory over the Texas Rangers.

Shockingly, the four division winners in 1985, Los Angeles, St. Louis, Kansas City and Toronto, were out of the running early and never made a serious threat to repeat. Of the four teams, only Toronto was able to play over .500 ball in 1986.

Here are the final standings in 1986.

AMERICAN LEAGUE

EAST	Won	Lost	Pct.	GB
Boston Red Sox	95	66	.590	
New York Yankees	90	72	.556	5.5
Detroit Tigers	87	75	.537	8.5
Toronto Blue Jays	86	76	.531	9.5
Cleveland Indians	84	78	.519	11.5
Milwaukee Brewers	77	84	.478	18
Baltimore Orioles	73	89	.451	22.5
WEST	**Won**	**Lost**	**Pct.**	**GB**
California Angels	92	70	.568	
Texas Rangers	87	75	.537	5
Kansas City Royals	76	86	.469	16
Oakland A's	76	86	.469	16
Chicago White Sox	72	90	.444	20
Minnesota Twins	71	91	.438	21
Seattle Mariners	67	95	.414	25

NATIONAL LEAGUE

EAST	Won	Lost	Pct.	GB
New York Mets	108	54	.667	
Philadelphia Phillies	86	75	.534	21.5
St. Louis Cardinals	79	82	.491	28.5
Montreal Expos	78	83	.484	29.5
Chicago Cubs	70	90	.438	37
Pittsburgh Pirates	64	98	.395	44
WEST	**Won**	**Lost**	**Pct.**	**GB**
Houston Astros	96	66	.593	
Cincinnati Reds	86	76	.531	10
San Francisco Giants	83	79	.512	13
San Diego Padres	74	88	.457	22
Los Angeles Dodgers	73	89	.451	23
Atlanta Braves	72	89	.447	23.5

The batting titles in each league went down to the final weekend before the champion was decided. In the American League, Wade Boggs and Don Mattingly battled the whole month of September and October before Boggs edged Mattingly. Boggs, however, was injured the final weekend with a hamstring problem and didn't play. In the senior circuit, Tim Raines, Steve Sax and Tony Gwynn all went into the final few days of play with a chance to capture the crown. Raines, a free agent, edged Sax and Gwynn to win his first title.

There was little doubt who would win the N.L.'s home run championship as Mike Schmidt, the league's Most

Valuable Player, cracked 37, six more than second-place finishers Glenn Davis and Dave Parker. Schmidt also won the RBI crown by knocking in three more than Parker with 119.

The American League's home run and RBI leaders were both surprises. Jessie Barfield, the Toronto outfielder, belted a career-high 40 home runs to outdistance Dave Kingman. Cleveland's Joe Carter took the runs batted in title also with a career-high. Carter knocked in 121 runs, nipping Oakland rookie Jose Canseco by four.

There was no surprise in the stolen base titleists for either league as the chalk, Rickey Henderson in the

Barfield (above) also knocked in a career-high 108 runs, placing him fifth in the A.L. The Reds' Eric Davis (facing page) exploded onto the scene by cracking 27 home runs and finishing second to Vince Coleman in stolen bases with 80.

A.L. and Vince Coleman in the N.L. easily defended their titles. Henderson swiped 87 bags for the Yankees while Coleman stole 107, the first time a player has ever stolen over 100 bases in each of his first two seasons in the game.

Here are the leaders on offense.

AMERICAN LEAGUE

BATTING AVERAGE

Wade Boggs	Boston	.357
Don Mattingly,	New York	.352
Kirby Puckett,	Minnesota	.328
Pat Tabler,	Cleveland	.326
Jim Rice,	Boston	.324
Robin Yount,	Milwaukee	.312
Tony Fernandez,	Toronto	.310
Phil Bradley,	Seattle	.310
George Bell,	Toronto	.309
Julio Franco,	Cleveland	.306

HOME RUNS

Jessie Barfield	Toronto	40
Dave Kingman	Oakland	35
Gary Gaetti	Minnesota	34
Jose Canseco	Oakland	33
Rob Deer	Milwaukee	33
Don Baylor	Boston	31
George Bell	Toronto	31
Don Mattingly	New York	31
Kirby Puckett	Minnesota	31
Pete Incaviglia	Texas	30

RUNS BATTED IN

Joe Carter	Cleveland	121
Jose Canseco	Oakland	117
Don Mattingly	New York	113
Jim Rice	Boston	110
Jessie Barfield	Toronto	108
George Bell	Toronto	108
Gary Gaetti	Minnesota	108
Wayne Presley	Seattle	107
Dave Winfield	New York	104
Bill Buckner	Boston	102

STOLEN BASES

Rickey Henderson	New York	87
John Cangelosi	Chicago	50
Gary Pettis	California	50
Kirk Gibson	Detroit	34
Willie Wilson	Kansas City	34
Alfredo Griffin	Oakland	33
Oddibe McDowell	Texas	33
Brett Butler	Cleveland	32
Lloyd Moseby	Toronto	32
Jerry Reynolds	Seattle	30

NATIONAL LEAGUE

BATTING AVERAGES

Tim Raines	Montreal	.334
Steve Sax	Los Angeles	.332
Tony Gwynn	San Diego	.329
Kevin Bass	Houston	.311
Keith Hernandez	New York	.310
Von Hayes	Philadelphia	.305
Johnny Ray	Pittsburgh	.301
Ray Knight	New York	.298
Mitch Webster	Montreal	.290
Mike Schmidt	Philadelphia	.290

HOME RUNS

Mike Schmidt	Philadelphia	37
Glenn Davis	Houston	31
Dave Parker	Cincinnati	31
Dale Murphy	Atlanta	29
Eric Davis	Cincinnati	27
Bob Horner	Atlanta	27
Darryl Strawberry	New York	27
Kevin McReynolds	San Diego	26
Gary Carter	New York	24

RUNS BATTED IN

Mike Schmidt	Philadelphia	119
Dave Parker	Cincinnati	116
Gary Carter	New York	105
Glenn Davis	Houston	101
Von Hayes	Philadelphia	98
Kevin McReynolds	San Diego	96
Darryl Strawberry	New York	93
Jim Morrison	Pittsburgh	88
Bob Horner	Atlanta	87
Candy Maldonado	SanFrancisco	85

STOLEN BASES

Vince Coleman	St. Louis	107
Eric Davis	Cincinnati	80
Tim Raines	Montreal	70
Mariano Duncan	Los Angeles	48
Bill Doran	Houston	42
Juan Samuel	Philadelphia	42
Steve Sax	Los Angeles	40
Billy Hatcher	Houston	38
Tony Gwynn	San Diego	37

Facing page: Mattingly and Boggs.

43

Glenn Davis (facing page) finished second in homers with 31. Gary Carter (above) knocked in 105 runs while Darryl Strawberry (left) had 97. Jim Rice (right) batted .324.

From the start of the season, there was no doubt that Roger Clemens was the standout pitcher in the American League. He struck out 20 Mariners to set the major league record for strikeouts in a game and by season's end had captured the earned run average title with a 2.48. Dave Righetti paced the A.L.'s firemen by registering a record 46 saves.

In the National League, not only did Mike Scott of the Astros pitch a no-hitter to sew up the West Division for Houston, but also took the e.r.a. championship. Rookie Todd Worrell of St. Louis edged veteran reliever Jeff Reardon of Montreal for the saves title with 36.

Here are the pitching leaders of 1986.

AMERICAN LEAGUE

EARNED RUN AVERAGE

Roger Clemens	Boston	2.48
Ted Higuera	Milwaukee	2.79
Mike Witt	California	2.84
Bruce Hurst	Boston	2.99
Danny Jackson	Kansas City	3.20
Jack Morris	Detroit	3.27
Kirk McCaskill	California	3.36
Curt Young	Oakland	3.45
Floyd Bannister	Chicago	3.54
Tom Candiotti	Cleveland	3.57

NATIONAL LEAGUE

EARNED RUN AVERAGE

Mike Scott	Houston	2.22
Bob Ojeda	New York	2.57
Ron Darling	New York	2.81
Rick Rhoden	Pittsburgh	2.84
Dwight Gooden	New York	2.84
Danny Cox	St. Louis	2.90
John Tudor	St. Louis	2.92
Mike Krukow	San Francisco	3.05
Scott Garrelts	San Francisco	3.11
Bob Knepper	Houston	3.14

SAVES

Dave Righetti	New York	46
Don Aase	Baltimore	34
Tom Henke	Toronto	27
Willie Hernandez	Detroit	24
Donnie Moore	California	21
Greg Harris	Texas	20
Ernie Camacho	Cleveland	19
Mark Clear	Milwaukee	16
Jay Howell	Oakland	16
Bob Stanley	Boston	16

SAVES

Todd Worrell	St. Louis	36
Jeff Reardon	Montreal	35
Dave Smith	Houston	33
Lee Smith	Chicago	31
Steve Bedrosian	Philadelphia	29
John Franco	Cincinnati	29
Gene Garber	Atlanta	24
Roger McDowell	New York	22
Rich Gossage	San Diego	21
Jessie Orosco	New York	21

Gooden (facing page), Coleman (top right)
and Dave Smith (top left).

THE NATIONAL LEAGUE

EAST

NEW YORK METS

The New York Mets' ride along Broadway as World Champions in October should have come as no surprise to baseball followers. After all, this was a team that won more games the previous two seasons than any other team in the game – and still didn't make the playoffs. But this Mets squad made sure there were no errors, no close calls that might have prevented them from their quest. And, barring any unforseen difficulties, the Mets are the team to beat in 1987.

In the offseason of '85, the Mets only made one big trade, but that turned out to be a tremendous shot in the arm. New York received Bob Ojeda, the lefthander the New Yorkers needed to combat the Cardinals' speed, in return for a bevy of players. All Ojeda did was become the Mets' most consistent hurler, winning 18 games, losing 5 and finishing second in the National League in earned run average with 2.57. He also helped the Mets staff lead the league as a team, finishing ahead of the West Division champions Houston Astros.

Ojeda had lots of help on the mound as Ron Darling, Dwight Gooden and Sid Fernandez combined to give the Mets the best starting rotation in baseball. Darling won 15 games, Gooden 17 and Fernandez 16, while Rick Aguilera, the fifth starter, won 10 games.

The bullpen was just as solid as Roger McDowell became the number one man and won 14 games, saved 22 and proved to have a rubber arm, appearing in 75 games and 128 innings. Jessie Orosco overcame early difficulties to finish with 21 saves and a 2.33 e.r.a.

Gary Carter (previous main) led the Mets to the Series and Pete Rose (inset) added to his hits record. Sid Fernandez (facing page) blossomed into an All-Star, winning 16 games for New York. Dwight Gooden and Carter (right) celebrate one of Doc's 18 victories.

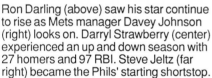

Ron Darling (above) saw his star continue to rise as Mets manager Davey Johnson (right) looks on. Darryl Strawberry (center) experienced an up and down season with 27 homers and 97 RBI. Steve Jeltz (far right) became the Phils' starting shortstop.

The hitting was just as successful as the pitching staff, as New York led the league in team batting with a .263 average. Keith Hernandez and Gary Carter had typical seasons, but Len Dykstra and Wally Backman emerged to add spunk and tenacity at the top of the lineup. Ray Knight, thought to be finished at spring training, rebounded magnificently, winning the World Series MVP after hitting .298 in the regular season.

The Mets are talented and young. Another ride down Broadway is a good bet.

PHILADELPHIA PHILLIES

It took Philadelphia a while, but they finally found their stride at midseason. Unfortunately, by that time, the Mets were already romping with a 20-plus game lead on the rest of the East.

Hitting has never been a problem for Philadelphia as long as Mike Schmidt's been there. Schmidt captured his third National League Most Valuable Player award last season by hitting .290 with 37 homers and 119 RBI. He also had lots of help

from a team placed second in the N.L. in home runs with 154.

Von Hayes finally blossomed as the player Philadelphia expected when they traded five players for him. Hayes had his best season, hitting .305 with 19 home runs and 98 RBI. Besides Hayes and Schmidt, other big bats belonged to Glenn Wilson (.271, 15 HR, 84 RBI) and Juan Samuel (.266, 16 HR, 78 RBI).

The problem with the Phillies was on the hill. Shane Rawley became an All-Star but, soon after the mid-season classic, developed a bad shoulder

ST. LOUIS CARDINALS

There was no team in baseball that experienced more frustration and disappointment than the St. Louis Cardinals. A year removed from coming up one game shy of the world championship, the Cardinals plummetted to third in the East, 28½ games behind the division-winning Mets and three games under the .500 mark.

After leading the National League in batting in 1985, the Cardinals' bats collectively went cold, finishing last as a team with a .236 average. They hit fewer home runs (58) as a club in '86 than Roger Maris did as an individual in 1961. The big boomers from the pennant year, Jack Clark, Tommy Herr and Willie McGee, sputtered badly due to injury (in Clark's case) or simply a poor year. McGee hit nearly 100 points lower than the previous season, when he was the N.L. batting champion and Most Valuable Player. Herr, who hit over .300 with more than 100 RBI in '85, dropped to .252 with only 61 runs batted in. And Clark, the only real power bat in the lineup, started slowly, then injured a thumb and played in only 65 games. To put everything in perspective, the Cardinals' leading hitter was Ozzie Smith, who batted .280, and who is paid $2M a year for his superb glove.

The hitting wasn't the sole cause of the Cards' demise. The pitching, which figured prominently the year before, placed fourth in the league in earned run average (3.32), but it also was hurt by injuries.

The biggest blow to the staff was in the bullpen. Jeff Lahti, the team leader in saves, hurt his arm in spring training and missed virtually the whole season, not registering one save. The lefty out of the pen, Ken Dayley, was hampered throughout the year with arm troubles and his effectiveness was limited.

All was not morbid in the bullpen, though, as Todd Worrell shot to stardom with a blazing fastball that helped him set a rookie record with 36 saves. His performance (nine wins with a 2.08 e.r.a.) earned him the league's Rookie of the Year award.

If the Cards are to be a factor in the race, the pitching staff will need to stay healthy. But most of all, the hitters will have to return to the form of 1985.

Mike Schmidt (facing page and overleaf top right inset) and Todd Worrell (above) were leaders on the Phils and Cards, respectively. Vince Coleman (overleaf main) led baseball in SBs. Bottom inset: Juan Samuel of the Phils.

which prematurely ended his season. When Rawley went down it brought young Bruce Ruffin to the forefront, and Ruffin impressed everyone with his poise and control. The rookie southpaw won nine games, lost only four and compiled an impressive 2.46 e.r.a.

The only other reliable starter was Don Carman, who was transported from the bullpen. Carman finished the season strongly, ending up with a 10-5 record and a 3.22 e.r.a. Kevin Gross, a big surprise in '85, fell off form, winning 12 games but finishing with an e.r.a of 4.02. The reason Carman was shipped from the pen was the arrival of Steve Bedrosian.

Bedrosian came to Philadelphia in an off-season trade from Atlanta and quickly became the stopper. Bedrock ended the season with an 8-6 record, a 3.39 e.r.a and a career-high 29 saves.

The Phillies are a young, fast, power-hitting team that could use pitching to take it over the top. If it gets any, the Mets and the rest of the National League better beware.

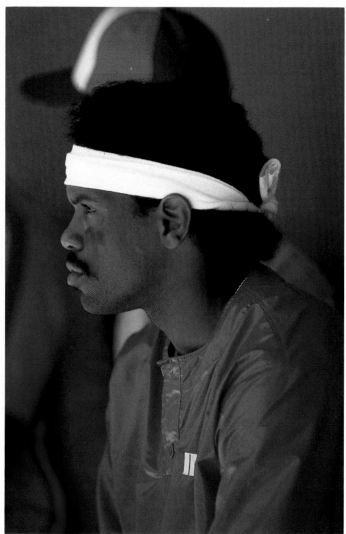

MONTREAL EXPOS

For the first half of the 1986 season, the only team that had a shot at overtaking the New York Mets in the East was Montreal. Bolstered by a strong hitting attack led by Hubie Brooks, Tim Raines and Andre Dawson, the Expos stayed close through May. But then came June.

In that month, Brooks went down with a serious thumb injury that eventually sidelined him for the rest of the season. Until that point, the ex-Mets shortstop was in contention for the Triple Crown, batting .340 with 14 home runs, 58 RBI and 10 game-winning RBI. But as soon as Brooks was lost, the Expos faltered.

They fell from less than 10 games off the lead to finishing 29 ½ games behind, and their record dropped under .500 to 78-83. And as their record dropped, so did their attendance, with Montreal only

Tim Raines (above right and left) and Andre Dawson (facing page) won't be returning to the Expos. Hubie Brooks' (left) season was ended by injuries.

outdrawing Pittsburgh in the National League in home sales.

But you can expect the Expos attendance and their performance to drop even further if would-be free agents, Raines and Dawson, decide to take a hike. Raines merely led the league in batting with a .334 mark and finished third in stolen bases with 70. Dawson, though hampered for much of the season with injuries, still managed to hit .284 with 20 home runs and 78 RBI.

Injuries really hurt the Montreal pitching staff when Joe Hesketh, a prize rookie a year before, was lost for a season with an arm injury. Bryn Smith, Montreal's leading hurler in '85,

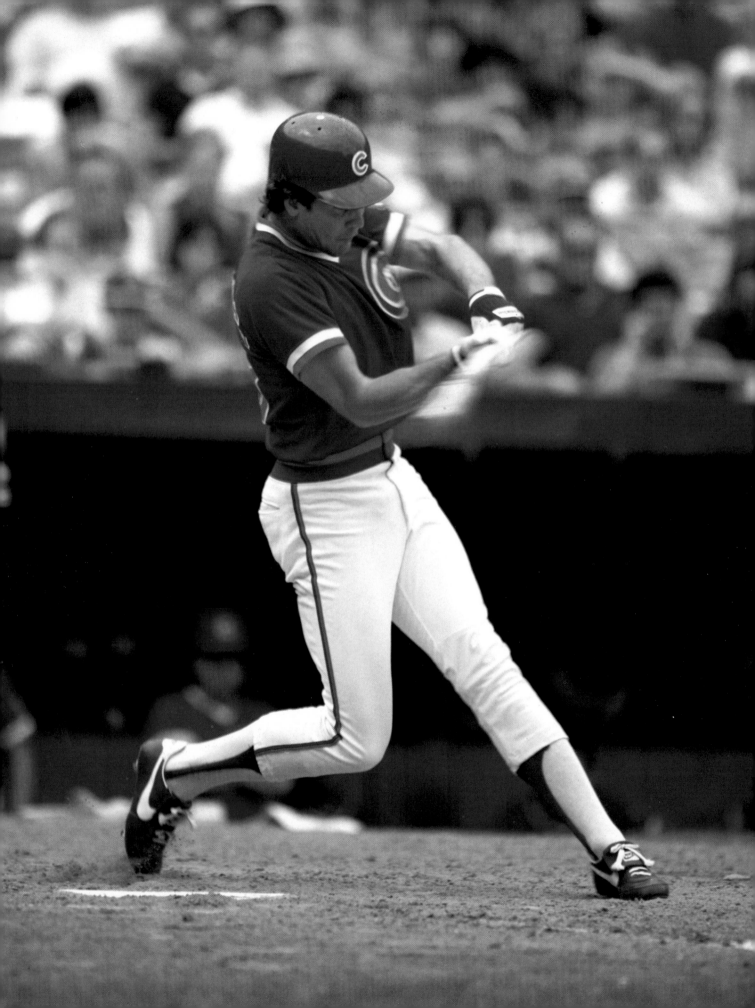

helped compound matters by having a poor season, winning only 10 games and posting an earned run average of 3.94. The bullpen was dependable as usual, with Jeff Reardon registering 35 saves and seven wins. Reardon was bolstered by fine performances from Tim Burke (9-7, 2.93) and Andy McGaffigan (10-5, 2.65). The surprise of the staff was the continued development of Floyd Youmans, the former high school teammate of Dwight Gooden. Youmans started slowly, but came on strong to win 13 games and average nearly a strikeout per inning.

But for the Expos to contend in 1987, they'll have to shore up the starting pitching and hope Raines and Dawson decide they like the Canadian climate.

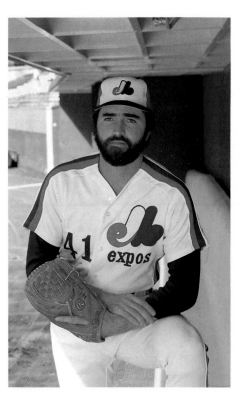

Ryne Sandberg (facing page and below left and right) starred for Chicago while reliever Jeff Reardon is now a Minnesota Twin.

CHICAGO CUBS

Ever since the Cubs lost that final game in the 1984 League Championship Series to San Diego, they've been a team doing a free fall. Two seasons ago, they finished 23 ½ games behind the Cardinals, although many experts attributed that to massive injuries. But last seaon they fell 37 games from the top and there was only one reason – the Cubs are a bad baseball team.

And the worst part of the club was the pitching staff. Chicago placed dead last in the N.L. in pitching, yielding an average of 4.49 runs per nine innings. They were also the only team in the league to post an e.r.a. of over 4.00. Not one pitcher compiled an e.r.a. of under 3.00 and, incredibly, not one managed to win at least 10 games.

The main culprit on the staff was Rick Sutcliffe. Only two years ago Sutcliffe won the Cy Young award and translated that into a million-dollar-a-

Tony Pena (facing page) and Johnny Ray (above) show the form that made them the offensive leaders for the last-place Pittsburgh Pirates.

registered solid numbers at the plate (.250, 21 HR, 74 RBI).

For the Cubs to contend this season, general manager Dallas Green will have to import some quality pitching talent. The only problem is that he doesn't have anything anybody else wants to use in a trade.

PITTSBURGH PIRATES

You might say that, in 1986, the Pirates won the war but lost the battle. Sure, the city of Pittsburgh was able to save a team that nearly left town. And sure, the Pirates did manage to attract more than 1,000,000 fans to Three Rivers Stadium. Equally sure, the fans who did show up were privy to some pretty bad baseball.

The Pirates finished 44 games behind the Mets and were the only team in baseball not to play .400 ball. Their hitting placed next to last in the league, batting a collective .250, and the pitching staff was not much better.

But while the numbers were bad, the future looks better for the Bucs. Barry Bonds emerged last season as a legitimate threat in the batters box and on the basepaths. The son of former star Bobby Bonds, Barry belted 16 home runs and knocked in 48 runs in only 113 games. Although he batted only .223, when he did get on base he was a terror, stealing 36 bags. Johnny Ray continued to be an overlooked star as he batted .301 with seven homers and 78 RBI, very respectable numbers for a second baseman. Jim Morrison, a journeyman most of his career, received a chance to start and made the best of it, smashing 23 homers, driving in 88 runs and hitting .274.

Perhaps the reason the Pirates lost so many games was their bullpen. The Bucs had the worst record in the league in one-run games (16-37) and finished below .500 in extra-inning affairs (7-10). But they may have found an answer to their bullpen woes when they dealt for reliever Brian Fisher (and a solid young starter, Doug Drabek) in the offseason.

If the Pirates youngsters continue to develop and the pitching staff can find a stopper, the Bucs may be a more formidable squad in 1987. At least they may find their way out of the cellar.

year contract. Last season, Sutcliffe's record was 5-14 with an e.r.a. of 4.64. Joining Sutcliffe on the most disappointing list were Dennis Eckersley (6-11, 4.57) and Steve Trout (5-7, 4.75). The only player who put respectable numbers on the board was relief ace Lee Smith, who posted 31 saves while winning nine games, tops on the staff.

Despite the awful pitching, the hitting was just fine. The Cubs finished third in the league in batting with a .256 average and hit the most home runs. Though no Cubs player hit higher than .300, Ryne Sandberg (.284, 14 home runs, 76 RBI and 34 stolen bases) and Keith Moreland (.271, 12 HR, 79 RBI) had fine seasons. Jody Davis once again proved to be a workhorse behind the dish as he played in 148 games and

While the hitting was just fine, the pitching was even better. The Astros' staff finished second behind the Mets in team pitching with a 3.11 earned run average. Mike Scott, whose split-fingered fastball drove hitters crazy, won the Cy Young award, winning 18 games and leading the league in strikeouts with 306 and e.r.a. with a 2.22. Bob Knepper continued to be a solid starter, winning 17 games, while Nolan Ryan pitched through pain the second half of the season and won 12 games overall. The pitcher to watch on the staff, though, is Jim Deshaies. A rookie a year ago, Deshaies compiled a 12-5 record with a 3.25 e.r.a. This season, expect Deshaies to blossom and become one of the league's best southpaw starters.

The Houston bullpen was more than adequate. Dave Smith saved 33 games and Charlie Kerfeld provided comic relief and an exploding fastball as Smith's set-up man.

The Astros that won 96 games in 1986 were no fluke. A 100-win season in '87 wouldn't be out of the question.

CINCINNATI REDS

Before the season began, Pete Rose's Reds were considered by some the team to beat in the N.L. West. Bolstered by acquisitions to the pitching staff of Bill Gullickson and John Denny, the Reds felt they had the talent to take them over the top.

Things did not develop as expected in Cincinnati. The Reds began the season horribly, falling behind the pack early with a long losing streak at home. And until they could straighten themselves out, the race was all but over for the Reds.

The pitching staff never reached the potential Rose felt they would attain as both Gullickson and Denny faltered. By season's end, Gullickson did improve, but the Reds still finished with the fourth worst earned run average. Tom Browning, who won 20 games as a rookie in 1985, suffered through an off-season, winning 14

WEST

HOUSTON ASTROS

Perhaps no team in baseball took a faster turn for the better than the Houston Astros. When Hal Lanier was hired as manager of the Astros, he promised that the team would be more aggressive than the Punch and Judy teams of the past. Not only did Lanier deliver a more exciting, more aggressive team to Houston, but he also brought a division title for the first time since 1980.

For his assertive direction, Lanier took National League honors as manager of the year and came within a couple of breaks of bringing Houston to the World Series.

Lanier did have plenty of tools to work with. He realized that the Astros had plenty of speed and he used it often as Houston finished third in the N.L. in stolen bases. He also had an advantage no other Astro skipper has had in the recent past – a power hitter. Glenn Davis provided Houston with their first legitimate clean-up hitter since Jimmy Wynn. Davis belted 31 homers and knocked in 101 runs to place second behind Philadelphia's Mike Schmidt in the MVP voting.

Besides Davis, Kevin Bass developed into an All-Star, batting .311 with 20 home runs and 79 RBI while Denny Walling had his best season in the majors, hitting .312 with 13 homers and 58 RBI in limited playing time. But the catalyst for the Astros was second baseman Bill Doran, who batted .276 and stole 42 bags.

Kevin Bass (facing page) and Charlie Kerfeld (above) were two of the reasons the Houston Astros surprisingly won the West Division.

Glenn Davis (main picture) developed into one of the National League's best power hitters, clouting 31 homers and driving in 101 runs for the Astros. Nolan Ryan (inset) rebounded from an arm injury and pitched effectively.

with an e.r.a of 3.81. And Ted Power, the right-handed ace out of the bullpen, was so horrible in relief (he saved only one game in '86, compared to 27 a year before), that Rose had to move him to the starting rotation. One of the few bright spots on the staff was the work of John Franco out of the pen. Franco came on to save 29 games and post an e.r.a of under 3.00 in 74 appearances.

But all was not bad for the Reds. Eric Davis, who has been on the threshold of stardom for two years, finally emerged in a big way. The 24-year-old centerfielder started slowly then hit his stride at midseason to become one of the big stories in '86. Davis batted .277 with 27 home runs, 71 runs batted in and 80 stolen bases in just 415 at-bats. He was aided on offense by Dave Parker (.273, 31 HR, 116 RBI) and a resurgent Buddy Bell (.278, 20 HR, 75 RBI).

There's no doubt that the Reds

Dave Parker (above right) and Eric Davis (facing page bottom) led the Reds offense while John Franco (above right) was the stopper. Jeffrey Leonard (facing page top) collides at home plate.

---

will score a lot of runs in 1987. Now, if they could find a couple of pitchers to stop the opposition, the Reds may give Houston a good run for the West division title.

SAN FRANCISCO GIANTS

One of the nicest stories in baseball last season was the resurgence of the San Francisco Giants franchise. A year earlier, the Giants were in disarray, losing 100 games for the first time since they moved to San Francisco. There was talk that the Giants were

ready to move from San Francisco to San Jose. But in the offseason the Giants hired Roger Craig to manage and the fortunes of the franchise turned around.

The Giants were in contention for most of the year and actually posted a record of better than .500 (83-79). Craig, the master of the split-fingered fastball, tutored most of the Giants' pitchers and the result was the third-best staff in the league. Leading the staff was Mike Krukow, who not only was a member of the All-Star team, but also won 20 games for the first time in his career. Scott Garrelts shifted from the bullpen to the starting staff, then back to the pen, and won 13 games while saving 10.

One area that certainly helped save the Giants was the offense. A unit that finished last in '85, the Giants' hitters rebounded in a big way in '86. The oft-injured Chris Brown led San Francisco in batting with a .317

Mike Krukow (inset left) became a 20-game winner thanks to Roger Graig's (inset top) tutoring on the split-fingered fastball. Tony Gwynn (main picture) battled for the N.L. batting crown.

average and Chili Davis came back to his earlier form by hitting .278 with 13 homers and 70 runs batted in. The surprises came in the form of two rookies and a former bench player.

Rob Thompson, who jumped from Double A ball to the majors, stepped in and played a solid second base while hitting .271. His efforts helped him place second in the rookie of the year, balloting behind the Cardinals' Todd Worrell. Will Clark was not expected to start the season with the Giants, but a strong spring training persuaded Craig to bring Clark north. The Mississippi State graduate responded by hitting .287 with 11 HRs and 47 RBI. Candy Maldonado was traded to the Giants by the Dodgers and nobody expected him to be anything but a pinch-hitter. But when Jeff Leonard was injured, Maldonado took his spot and knocked in 85 runs with 18 homers.

With the young players growing up, the Giants franchise is more secure than in recent memory. Now if the young pitchers can develop as expected, the Giants won't be looking from the bottom up any more.

Both Fernando Valenzuela (top) and Steve Sax (above) had their best seasons for the Dodgers. San Diego rid inself in the offseason of infielder Jerry Royster (facing page top) and outfielder Kevin McReynolds (facing page bottom).

SAN DIEGO PADRES

There was no team in baseball that went through more turmoil last year than the Padres. Before the season even began, manager Dick Williams left the team on less than amicable terms. The departure of Williams, a notorious hard-liner, and the arrival of easy-going Steve Boros as skipper were applauded by many of the players. But by season's end the manager was fired, and players engaged in verbal sparring with the front office.

Outfield slugger Kevin McReynolds was benched at times and although he finished the year with outstanding statistics (.287, 26 HRs, 96 RBI), he was traded to the Mets for prospects. Early in the season, the front office refused to let players drink beer in the lockerroom after games, leaving Goose Gossage to rip management. But that was nothing compared to later in the season when the front office publicly stated that it would not attempt to sign free-agent Tim Raines (whose speed would have given the Padres the dimension they needed) because of his past problems with substance abuse.

Gossage ripped management again on its decision not to seek Raines and Gossage was subsequently suspended by the team for the remainder of the campaign. His suspension was lifted a couple of weeks later, but it was just a microcosm of the Padres in 1986. More turmoil than wins.

San Diego finished in fourth place in the West with a 74-88 record. While the hitting was more than adequate (the Padres placed second in the National League in batting) and Tony Gwynn once again proved he is among the top five players in baseball (he was third in the batting race with a .329 average), the pitching staff was a disaster. The Padres staff finished next to last in the e.r.a. race and the top winner posted only 10 victories.

San Diego has already begun building for the future by trading catcher Terry Kennedy (opening a spot for highly-touted Benito Santiago) and naming the fiery Larry Bowa as manager. But don't expect miracles. The best Padres fans can hope for this season is for management and the players to start to get along.

LOS ANGELES DODGERS

The fortunes of the Dodgers took a severe turn downward as early as spring training last year. While running to third and sliding awkwardly, Pedro Guerrero tore up his knee and was lost for several months. His departure from the lineup proved the start of Los Angeles downfall that plummeted the proud Dodger franchise to a fifth place finish in 1986.

Bill Madlock (above) and Dave Anderson (facing page) were just two of the Los Angeles Dodgers who were struck with injuries in 1986. Both had more than one stint on the disabled list.

Guerrero wasn't the only prominent Dodger to take an extended break because of injury. Starters like Mike Marshall, Mike Scioscia, Mariano Duncan, Bill

Madlock, Greg Brock and Ken Landreaux took turns on the disabled list at some time during the year. With so many offensive weapons out of the lineup, the Dodgers needed to have strong pitching and a solid defense to stay in contention in the West.

The pitching, as usual, was strong. Overall, the staff placed fifth in the league in earned run average with a mark of 3.76. Fernando Valenzuela finally won 20 games and had perhaps his best season in the major leagues. Orel Hershiser was not nearly the dominant pitcher he was a year before, but he still managed 14 victories. And Rick Honeycutt, a question mark early, rebounded from arm troubles to win 12 games. But while the starters were impressive, the relief corps provided anything but relief.

Tom Niedenfuer looked like he still remembered Jack Clark's game-winning home run off him in the sixth game of the League Championship Series. His performance was spotty at best and his partner out of the pen, Ken Howell, was even more inconsistent. The bullpen is certainly one of the areas the Dodgers will try to shore up in the offseason.

While the pitching was acceptable, the defense was the joke of the league. Los Angeles committed 181 errors, 38 more than any National League team. Even manager Tommy Lasorda couldn't be optimistic about that.

But you can be sure that with a healthy Guerrero and an improved defense, the Dodgers will once again be contenders for the title.

ATLANTA BRAVES

What can be said about the Atlanta Braves except that they are several years away from contenders status? Maybe the best thing is that the Braves' management knows this and is willing to wait for the results.

Before last season began, owner Ted Turner coaxed Bobby Cox out of Toronto to run the show and Cox in turn hired Chuck Tanner to be his manager. Tanner and Cox quickly realized that the Braves didn't have the talent to be immediate contenders so they decided youth was the way to go.

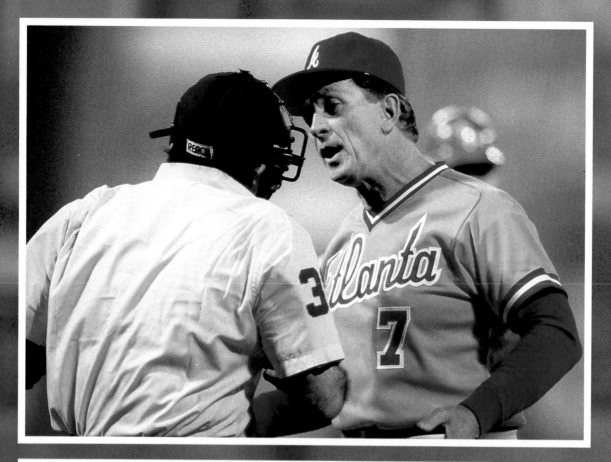

Orel Hershiser (inset top right) had a disappointing season for the Dodgers, while Braves' skipper Chuck Tanner (top) loses an argument. Ken Oberkfell (above) dives for a ball as teammate Andres Thomas (main) avoids a slide by Gary Carter.

The youth movement was felt mostly on the pitching staff, where four rookies received a chance to prove themselves at major league level. The best of the crop was Paul Assenmacher, a tall southpaw who prospered out of the bullpen. Assenmacher led the staff with a 2.50 earned run average and he compiled seven wins and seven saves in the process. While Assenmacher excited the Atlanta management with his bright future, 37-year-old Gene Garber came out of nowhere to anchor the bullpen after ace reliever Bruce Sutter was lost for the season with an arm injury. Garber became the number one fireman and registered 24 saves for the Braves.

The Atlanta offense proved to be a disappointment, and even the incomparable Dale Murphy suffered through an off-year. The two-time Most Valuable Player hit only .265 with 29 homers and 83 RBI. Nice numbers for most, but not for Murphy. Bob Horner was the Braves' best hitter, batting .273 with 27 home runs and 87 RBI. One player to watch on Atlanta is second year shortstop Andres Thomas. The slick-fielding Dominican showed flashes of brilliance last year

Atlanta's Dale Murphy (above and facing page top) suffered through an offseason by his standards, hitting only .265 with 29 homers and 83 RBI. Bob Horner (facing page bottom) hit 27 homers then opted for free agency.

and he could develop into a top-flight player.

The Braves know that they are destined to remain near or at the bottom in the N.L. West. But at least they'll be losing with youth – and an eye toward the future.

THE
★ AMERICAN ★
LEAGUE

EAST

BOSTON RED SOX

When the Boston Red Sox staked themselves to a big early lead in the East, fans around the country felt it was only a matter of time before the Sox ignominious history caught up with them and they fell from the top. Those fans waited and waited and waited, but the great fall never arrived. And if there was one player to thank most for the Red Sox division-winning campaign, it was pitcher Roger Clemens.

20-strikeout performance against Seattle early in the season was a new major league record and it was Clemens who provided the Sox with a win when they needed it most.

Clemens did have some help on the improved Boston staff. Bruce Hurst emerged to have an outstanding season, winning 13 games with a 2.99 e.r.a. and he gave the Mets fits in the World Series. Oil Can Boyd pitched well when he wasn't being suspended by Boston, and the Red Sox finally seemed to find a stopper in the bullpen when Calvin Schiraldi came up big late in the season. His poor World Series performance (he lost the last two games to New York) hopefully won't

Robin Yount (previous main) and Pete Incaviglia (inset) gave their team plenty of punch while Marty Barrett (right) developed into one of the A.L.'s best second baseman. Don Baylor (above) starred for the Sox.

set him back, but that merits watching in 1987.

The Red Sox have always had the bats and last season was no different. Wade Boggs won another batting title, his third in the last four years, by outhitting Don Mattingly, .357-.352. Jim Rice had an MVP-type season, hitting .324 with 20 homers and 110 RBI, and finished third behind Clemens and Mattingly in the balloting.

One of the main cogs for the Sox in '86 was the play of designated hitter Don Baylor. When Baylor came over from the Yankees in spring training,

The righthanded Clemens dazzled the baseball world like Dwight Gooden had the year before by posting a 24-4 record, an earned run average of 2.48 and taking the American League Cy Young award and Most Valuable Player award. His

not only did he inject a powerful righthanded bat into the lineup, but he provided an intangible in the clubhouse.

Boston is in line to make another strong run at the East Division title. They know they'll have the hitting. Once again, pitching will tell the story.

NEW YORK YANKEES

When the 1986 season ended and the trading season began, there was one area George Steinbrenner knew he had to improve if the Yankees were to take the East once again – pitching.

For in 1986, the Yankee pitching staff looked like a foxhole that was bombed by the enemy. Injuries and age took a toll on the staff as the Yanks used 19 pitchers during the

season. Their 4.11 earned run average placed them near the bottom of the league. Ron Guidry looked like he lost his lightning somewhere and Joe Niekro's performance proved the Yankees released the wrong Niekro in spring training. Brian Fisher, a tremendous addition to the bullpen in '85 as a rookie, fell on hard times and pitched to an e.r.a. of 4.93.

But not to worry. Even before the winter meetings, Steinbrenner packaged his good, young prospects for another old pitcher to help the staff. Gone were Fisher and Doug

_____

Boston's Wade Boggs (facing page) won another batting crown, nipping Don Mattingly, while Boggs' teammate Oil Can Boyd (below left) got into trouble again. Dave Winfield (below right) was chastised by George Steinbrenner for a slow start.

Drabek (who pitched well after a midseason recall, winning seven games) for veterans Rick Rhoden, Cecilio Guante and Pat Clements.

And all was not bad on the pitching staff. Dave Righetti took over as the best relief pitcher in baseball, saving a major league record 46 saves, winning eight games and registering a 2.45 e.r.a.

Once again the Yankee bats were harmful to American League e.r.a.'s. They finished second in the A.L. in batting with a .271 average. Don Mattingly continued to be the best hitter in baseball, combining a high average (.352) with enormous power (31 homers, 113 RBI). Mike Easler was a welcome addition as he hit over .300 with 14 homers and 78 RBI.

Dave Winfield overcame a rough start, a few benchings and being

chastised by Steinbrenner, to hit .262 with 24 HRs and 104 RBI. The player to watch this season is young Dan Pasqua. The lefthanded hitting outfielder batted .293 with 16 HRs and 45 RBI in only 280 at bats.

There's no question that the Yankees will hit in 1987. If they could find some decent pitching, New York should challenge for the top spot in the East.

DETROIT TIGERS

If there's one thing that could be said about the Tigers, it's that they can hit. Detroit led the major leagues in hitting home runs in '86, having six players clout 20 or more. But this could be a completely different squad by opening day. Two of the best players on the club, catcher Lance Parrish and pitcher Jack Morris, have applied for free agency and if either signs with another team, the Tigers will lose much of their bite.

Morris has been one of the premier pitchers of this decade and his record last season, 21-8 with a 3.27 earned run average, was a good indication of his importance to the Tigers. Parrish, on the other hand, is the mainstay behind the plate, a guy the pitching staff depends on to call the signals and the offense counts on to supply some punch. Parrish had an injury-riddled campaign a year ago, but still managed to hit .257 with 22 round-trippers and 62 runs batted in. Losing Parrish or Morris would push Detroit into the bottom half of this division.

There's no question that Detroit has a powerful lineup. Alan Trammell (.277, 21 HR, 75 RBI) and Lou Whitaker (20 HR, 73 RBI) were the only shortstop-second baseman combination to each hit over 20 homers. Kirk Gibson came back from an early injury to flash fine numbers, belting 28 homers, driving in 86 runs and stealing 34 bases, and Darrell Evans chipped in with 29 homers and 85 runs batted in.

On the hill, the Tigers were not a very solid group after Morris. Walt Terrell did win 15 games and Frank Tanana came off the scrap heap to win 12, but after that the rotation was suspect. In the pen, Willie Hernandez continues to be effective, saving 24 games and winning eight.

But the fate of the Tigers in 1987 rests with management. Do they make

Don Mattingly (facing page) continued to tear up A.L. pitching by batting .352 with 31 homers and 113 RBI. Both Lance Parrish (above) and Ron Guidry (left) suffered sub-par seasons and then sought free agency.

Morris and Parrish offers that will keep them in Detroit? If they do, Detroit will be a decent team. If not, look out below.

TORONTO BLUE JAYS

The Toronto Blue Jays were the overwhelming favorites to win the American League East a year ago for good reason. In '85, the Blue Jays took the crown despite sub-par performances by many of their hitters. With everybody returning to form, the Jays and their strong pitching staff would return to the top.

But it never happened. Sure the hitting was in place. In fact, Toronto batters were among the fiercest in the league, placing fourth in the A.L. in average. The twin terrors on the Jays were George Bell and Jessie Barfield. Both pounded out terrific years, with Bell batting .309 with 31 homers and 108 runs batted in. All Barfield did was lead the majors in home runs with 40, knock in 108 runs and bat .289. Beli and Barfield also led the team in stolen bases, taking 15 and 13 bags each, respectively.

They were not the only ones. Tony Fernandez continued to develop and now he's considered to be one of the finest shortstops in the game. Fernandez led the team in hitting with a .310 average, and he added 10 homers and 65 RBI.

The problem, obviously, was on the hill. Dave Stieb, the anchor of the

The Blue Jays cast of stars included Damaso Garcia, Willie Upshaw (above, left and right, respectively), Jessie Barfield (left) and George Bell (facing page). The Indians' Joe Carter (overleaf) led the A.L. in RBI.

staff who took the league's earned run average title the previous season, faltered badly to compile his worst statistics since joining the Jays. Stieb's e.r.a shot from 2.48 in 1985 to 4.74. He won but seven of 19 decisions and he yielded 239 hits in only 205 innings. Dennis Lamp, a mainstay on the division-winning team, saw his record fall to 2-6 with a bloated 5.05 e.r.a.

The one area the Blue Jays were strong in was the bullpen. Tom Henke delivered excellent work as the number one guy out of the pen,

saving 27 games, winning nine and registering a 3.35 e.r.a. The surprise of the staff was the development of rookie Mark Eichhorn. All Eichhorn did was win 14 games in relief, save 10 and allow only 1.72 runs per nine innings. His numbers earned him third place in the rookie of the year voting behind Jose Canseco and Wally Joyner.

If the Blue Jays get their pitching staff together, there's no reason they can't return to their status as the East's best team. In fact, you can count on it.

CLEVELAND INDIANS

Can you imagine that the Cleveland Indians are one of the teams to watch in the '87 season? And rivals better watch them for a positive reason, not negative ones like in the past. For the first time in a very long while, the Indians have the talent to contend for the pennant.

A year ago, Cleveland compiled its first winning record since 1979, finishing with an 84-78 record. Most of the credit for the Indians' rise to the top should go to the front office, which put together a tremendous hitting squad (they led the major leagues in batting with a .271 average) with the help of trades.

When Cleveland traded eventual Cy Young winning pitcher Rick Sutcliffe to the Cubs in 1984, the deal was ridiculed. But two seasons later, baseball experts are saying that deal was a steal for Cleveland. The biggest part of the trade was obtaining power-hitting outfielder Joe Carter. Carter emerged as the best RBI man in baseball, knocking in 121 runs while batting .302 and driving 29 homers. His companion in the Sutcliffe trade, Mel Hall, also came through with a big year, batting .296 with 18 home runs and 77 RBI.

The biggest surprise in Cleveland was rookie Cory Snyder. The former Brigham Young University player stepped in midway through the season and belted 24 homers, drove in 69 runs and batted .272 in 416 at bats. Besides his hitting exploits, Snyder gives the Indians flexibility because of his ability to play any number of positions on defense.

The trouble with the Indians was on the pitching side. Cleveland finished third from the bottom in the

The Milwaukee Brewers were delighted by the work of their young staff, but even veteran Mark Clear (facing page) rebounded to have a solid season. Julio Franco's (above) strong bat helped the Indians lead the majors in hitting.

American League in earned run average, yielding 4.58 runs per nine innings. Only one hurler, Tom Candiotti (16-12, 3.57 e.r.a.), could muster an e.r.a of under 4.00. Still, there is optimism because the Tribe used six different rookies on the staff at some time in the season. If any develop into dependable major league pitchers, the Indians could put pressure on the other East contenders.

Even if they don't, though, it's nice to talk about Cleveland in a positive way for once.

MILWAUKEE BREWERS

Sure Milwaukee finished in sixth place with a 77-84 record, but like Cleveland, this is another team that bears watching – but for a different reason. Whereas the Indians prosper on terrific hitting, the Brewers emphasis is on the mound.

Last season the Brewers went to a youth movement on its staff and it paid off. Milwaukee finished with the fifth best pitching staff in the American

League as they ended the campaign with a 4.01 earned run average. The best hurler on the staff is Ted Higuera. The Dominican pitcher impressed everyone with a dominating performance in the All-Star game and finished the season 20-11 with a 2.79 e.r.a., second only in the league to Roger Clemens. Former manager George Bamberger (he quit at season's end) also gave former phenom Tim Leary a second chance and Leary responded by winning 12 games. Juan Nieves, at 21 years old, won 11 ball games and showed the potential to be a big winner.

The big surprise on the hill was the performance of rookie relief pitcher Dan Plesac. The southpaw took over as lefty ace of the pen, winning 10 games, saving 14 and keeping his e.r.a under 3.00. Another pleasant surprise out of the pen was Mark Clear. The former Red Sox hurler saved 16 games, compiled an e.r.a. of 2.20 and struck out more than a batter an inning.

There were surprises on offense, also. Rob Deer, acquired in an offseason deal with San Francisco, was given a chance to play on an everyday basis and blasted A.L. pitching. The righthanded slugger belted 33 homers, drove in 86 runs, but hit only .232. Robin Yount made a successful move from shortstop to the outfield and hit .312 to lead the team and finish sixth in the A.L. batting race.

For the Brewers to improve even more, the young pitching staff will have to continue to develop. The bet here is that it will.

BALTIMORE ORIOLES

The Baltimore Orioles were so bad last year, Earl Weaver had to wonder why he ever came out of retirement to manage this team. Not only was the hitting far from the top, but the pitching was horrible.

The Orioles finished the season dead last in the East, 22 ½ games behind the Red Sox with a record of 73-89. It was their worst record in 31 years. It got so bad that Baltimore management criticised their best player, Eddie Murray, who suffered through an off-year for him. All Murray did was bat .305 (that mark led the team), drill 17 homers and knock in 84

When Eddie Murray went down with an injury, the Orioles brought up Jim Traber (main picture), who filled the offensive gap with a booming bat. The Baltimore troubles started on the hill, where veterans like Scott McGregor (inset) suffered through sub-par seasons.

runs. A fine year for anybody else, but not for Murray.

The Orioles did receive their usual good season from Cal Ripken (his dad is the new Baltimore manager) who hit .282 with 25 homers and 81 runs batted in and Fred Lynn, who batted .287 with 23 homers and 67 RBI. Mike Young, a phenom in '85, fell off sharply in '86, hitting just .252 with nine HRs and 42 RBI. Catcher Rick Dempsey fell off so badly that the Orioles not only dropped him from their roster after the season, but traded for San Diego backstop Terry Kennedy, who should add some punch to the lineup.

Don Aase (above) shows the form that made him a top A.L. reliever in '86. Ted Higuera (facing page) finished second to Roger Clemens in the Cy Young voting, while teammate Rob Deer (right) belted 33 homers.

The main reason the Orioles fell long and hard was their pitching staff. The long-time strong suit of the team, the staff finished with the fifth worst earned run average in the league, bottoming out at 4.30. Mike Boddicker rebounded from a dreadful '85 to win 14 games, although his e.r.a of 4.70 was nothing to be proud of. Mike Flanagan, a former star, won seven of 18 decisions and found his e.r.a. to be 4.24. And Scott McGregor, another veteran who prospered in the past, was 11-15 with a 4.52 e.r.a. The lone bright spot on the staff was the work of relief specialist Don Aase. Aase was

outstanding early in the season, saving the All-Star game for the American League and finishing the campaign with 34 saves and a 2.98 e.r.a.

The once proud Orioles franchise seems to have hit bottom. And with so many strong teams in the East, a return to the glorious past will be a difficult feat.

WEST

CALIFORNIA ANGELS

Before the 1986 season began, there weren't many experts who thought the Angels would contend, let alone win the West. But California's veteran team mixed a terrific pitching staff with some timely hitting to take the division before losing in disappointing fashion to Boston in the playoffs.

The backbone of the Angels was their pitching. California finished second to Kansas City in team pitching, yielding 3.82 runs per nine innings. And there were many reasons for the Angels' fine standing. The main reason was Mike Witt. The righthander, who tossed a perfect game on the last day of the 1984 season, finished the campaign with an 18-10 record, a 2.84 e.r.a (third in the league behind Roger Clemens and Ted Higuera) and over 200 strikeouts. Witt's strong performance was supported by youngster Kirk McCaskill. The former hockey player with the Winnipeg Jets won 17 games, lost 10 and posted a 3.36 e.r.a. McCaskill also struck out over 200 batters and allowed only 207 hits in 246.1 innings of work.

There was more where that came from. John Candelaria rebounded from an early-season arm injury to compose a 10-2 mark with a team-leading 2.55 e.r.a. And ancient Don Sutton, who won his 300th game of

---

Reggie Jackson (below left) finished his Angels' career and moved on to Oakland. Gary Pettis (below right) and Bob Boone (facing page) were stalwarts in the Angels' divisional championship.

his career, closed out the season with 15 victories. The bullpen belonged in the capable hands of righty Donnie Moore, who fought arm trouble all season to register 21 saves and a 2.97 e.r.a.

The Angels were no slouch at the bat either, especially with the emergence of super rookie Wally Joyner. All Joyner did was replace a legend (Rod Carew) and lead the team in runs batted in (100) and game-winning hits (14). The slick-fielding first baseman also hit 22 homers and batted .290. Joyner had help on offense from third baseman Doug DeCinces, who hit .256 with 26 homers and 96 RBI, and leftfielder Brian Downing, who added 20 homers and 95 RBI. The Reggie Jackson era ended in California as Reggie hit .241 with 18 home runs and 58 RBI.

For the Angels to repeat, they'll have to continue to get superb

pitching. But California is an old team and unless they start replacing their vets with kids, the bottom could fall out at any time. It may not happen at once, but it could start this season.

TEXAS RANGERS

One thing you could say about the Texas Rangers is that they're an exciting team to watch. At any point of the game, a big lead or large deficit could diminish in a flash. But, despite the Rangers' inconsistency last season, they finished in second place in the West, a tribute to aggressive manager Bobby Valentine and his use of kids.

Mitch Williams (above) stepped in as a rookie and contributed immediately, while 38-year-old Charlie Hough (right) refused to knuckle under to age.

When Valentine took the Rangers helm in the offseason, he knew Texas had one of the worst pitching staffs in the league. He also knew they had developed some fine young talent in the minors. Instead of opting for veterans, Valentine turned his mound corps over to the youngsters and they responded.

Take, for instance, the plight of starter Bobby Witt. Witt has an exploding fastball, and in 157.2

The Rangers were a
scrappy team in 1986;
here (main picture)
squeezing the Blue Jays'
Kelly Gruber at the
second base bag.
Veterans like Darrell
Porter (inset top) and
Charlie Hough (inset
bottom) helped give the
young Rangers some
stability.

innings the righthander struck out 174 batters. But he also walked 143 hitters, an enormous total for that number of innings. Ed Correa was another example. The righthanded rookie won 12 games, lost 14 and had a 4.32 earned run average. He, too, was plagued by control problems, walking 126 men in 202.1 innings. Yet another rookie, Mitch Williams, a fireballing relief specialist, put together an 8-6 record with a very respectable e.r.a of 3.58 and eight saves. In 98 innings, Williams yielded 79 free passes. So, while Valentine won 87 games with his crew of kids, it was exciting in more ways than one.

One player who was exciting on offense was rookie slugger Pete Incaviglia. The Oklahoma State grad pounded out 30 homers and drove in 88 runs while batting .250. He wasn't the only one to star offensively. Pete O'Brien batted .290 with 23 HRs and 90 RBI, Larry Parrish hit .276 with 28 roundtrippers and 94 RBI, and second year player Oddibe McDowell hit .266, clouted 18 homers and stole 33 bases.

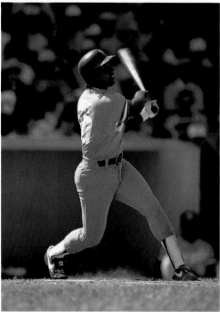

Bret Saberhagen (top) should be running for his life after a horrible season in '86. Frank White (above) continued to get better with age, while Willie Wilson (facing page) was a Royal catalyst.

If there is one thing you can say about Texas, it's that they're an exciting team to watch. And now, they're even winning.

KANSAS CITY ROYALS

There was no team in baseball that experienced a more horrible year than the Kansas City Royals. The World Champions of baseball finished the season in third place in the West, 16 games off the pace, with a dismal record of 76-86. But the most disastrous aspect of the season happened off the field.

Days after leading the American League past the Nationals in the All-Star game, manager Dick Howser complained of severe headaches and was checked into a hospital. Tests showed Howser had a brain tumor the size of a golf ball. Surgeons successfully removed the cancerous tumor, but things were never the same in Kansas City.

On the field, the Royals weren't the same team that pitched and hit

Mark Gubicza (below) pitched well while Donnie Hill tries to pitch around Mel Hall (main picture). Jose Canseco (inset top right) won the A.L. Rookie of the Year award for manager Tony LaRussa (inset bottom right).

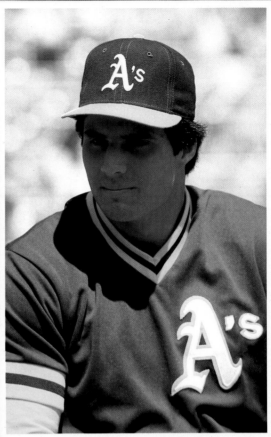

dominating as the previous season, still finished with the best e.r.a. in the league.

The offense, however, couldn't hold up its end. As a team, the Royals finished third from the bottom in batting, with a team average of only .252. The 137 homers as a team was the second worst in the league, as was the 12 shutouts against. George Brett, a huge force in the championship season, was knocked out by injuries again, playing 124 games and hitting .290 with only 73 RBI. With Brett having a poor season, Frank White tried to pick up the slack, belting 22 homers and driving in 84 runs while batting .272. Steve Balboni had a typical Balboni campaign, cracking 29 home runs, knocking in 88 runs and hitting just .229.

There's no doubt the Royals would like to forget the 1986 season. In more ways than one.

OAKLAND A'S

Looking at the statistics, it's amazing that the Oakland A's actually tied for third with the Royals and won 76 ballgames. Neither the offense, defense nor pitching finished anywhere near the top of the league.

But one thing the A's did have was Jose Canseco. The muscular, power-hitting outfielder won the American League's rookie of the year award by virtue of his outstanding numbers. The righthanded batter clouted 33 home runs, drove in 117 runs (second in the league behind Cleveland's Joe Carter) and hit .240. Canseco also knocked in 14 game-winning runs and showed his athletic ability by stealing 15 bases.

Veteran Dave Kingman joined Canseco in the power department by cracking 35 homers, driving in 94 runs and hitting a porous .210. Aside from those two, the only other real productive bats belonged to former batting champion Carney Lansford and shortstop Alfredo Griffin. The third baseman hit .284 with 19 dingers and 72 RBI. Griffin, meanwhile, led the regulars with a .285 average and stole a team-high 33 bases.

The pitching staff was the main problem. The A's used 20 hurlers during the season, five of them rookies. The team finished 10th in the league in earned run average with a

itself to a victory over the Cardinals in the World Series. Bret Saberhagen, the Cy Young winner of 1985, fell off considerably, and his record was 7-12 with a 4.15 earned run average. The rest of the staff, while not as

Harold Baines (above) proved to be one of the few bright spots on offense for the faltering White Sox. Bert Blyleven (facing page) continued to defy age as the 35-year-old led the A.L. in complete games.

mark of 4.31. The best pitcher on the staff, Moose Haas, was injured early, and former Cardinals ace Joaquin Andujar won only 12 games. The one bright spot on the mound corps was the development of lefty Curt Young, who placed seventh in the league in e.r.a. with a 3.45 grade.

The A's best hope is for Canseco to continue hitting home runs. At least then the fans will still show up.

MINNESOTA TWINS

The Twins have always been known as a squad that is built on hitting, not pitching. And that never came into focus any clearer than last season, as the Minnesota pitching staff was the worst in baseball.

Only one pitcher registered an earned run average of under 4.00. As a team, the Twins posted an e.r.a. of 4.77 and allowed more hits than any team in baseball except one. If there was an area of the staff that performed almost admirably, it was the starters. Burt Blyleven won 17 games and pitched 16 complete games. Frank Viola and Mike Smithson won 16 and 13 games, respectively. The major problem with the staff was in the bullpen.

Minnesota garnered the fewest saves of any team in baseball: 24. Not one reliever earned more than 10 saves. The bullpen was one of the reasons the Twins' starters completed 39 games, the most in the league.

Things were not as negative on the offense, where Minnesota hit the second highest number of homers in baseball. Kirby Puckett must have eaten Wheaties, as he clouted 31 homers, knocked in 96 runs and batted .328. The little leadoff hitter placed third in the league in batting and his 31 home runs was an improvement of 27 more than his first two seasons in the majors combined. His power numbers were one of the reasons the lively ball theory was such a hot topic during the summer.

Gary Gaetti also had a monster year, batting .287 with 34 homers and 108 RBI, while Kent Hrbek returned to form with 29 roundtrippers and 91 RBI. Rightfielder Tom Brunansky chipped in with 23 homers and 75 runs batted in while Roy Smalley added to the attack, cracking 20 dingers and 57 RBI.

Should the Twins develop a bullpen, a couple more dependable starters and Puckett's recipe for success, Minnesota will be a better team. But that's too much to ask any team in one offseason.

CHICAGO WHITE SOX

If you could select one reason why the Chicago White Sox finished a dismal fifth in the West with a 72-90 record (forgetting, of course, the turmoil surrounding former general manager Ken "Hawk" Harrelson) it would be the offense. In fact, the White Sox were very offensive during the 1986 season.

As a team, they finished dead last in batting, hitting only .247, almost 40 points lower than the league-leading Indians. The Sox finished with the fewest hits, fewest runs, fewest doubles, fewest home runs, fewest — well, you get the idea.

Only one player performed near his capabilities: Harold Baines. The perennial All-Star batted .296 with 21 home runs and 88 RBI. No other player had more than 63 RBI and no regular batted higher than .250 other than Baines. Carlton Fisk was a flop the year after hitting 37 homers as he batted .221 with 14 dingers.

The pitching staff had a fine year, and if the hitters could have scored some runs, the records of the hurlers might have been a lot better. As a team, the Sox placed third in the

Blyleven (facing page) should be sticking out his tongue considering the support he got from his teammates. Mike Moore (above) became a solid contributor to the Mariner rotation.

league in earned run average with a 3.93 mark. Jose DeLeon came over from the Pirates in a midseason trade and sparkled, allowing only 49 hits in 79 innings with an e.r.a. of 2.96. Floyd Bannister's record of 10-14 was nothing thrilling, but he did pitch well, as his 3.54 e.r.a. shows. Even Neil Allen, the former reliever, performed admirably, posting a 7-2 record with a 3.82 e.r.a. But the best performance of the season for the Sox was by Joe Cowley. Traded to the Sox for Britt Burns in the offseason, Cowley hurled a no-hitter and won more games (11) than any pitcher on the staff.

But for the Sox to be contenders in '87, they'll have to find some punch at the plate.

SEATTLE MARINERS

The Mariners had such high hopes for the 1986 season. Experts felt that not only would Seattle place in the upper half of the division, but they expected the Mariners to contend for the crown. But things fell apart quickly in the west.

The biggest problem the Mariners had was on the hill. Seattle finished next-to-last in baseball in earned run

Phil Bradley (left) flails away at a pitch, something the Mariners did a lot in breaking the A.L. record for team strikeouts. Frank Viola (above) was one of the few reliable starters for Minnesota.

average, with a bloated mark of 4.65. They allowed more hits than any team in baseball and compiled the fewest shutouts. Their best pitcher was Mark Langston, who registered a 12-14 mark with an e.r.a. of 4.85. Langston did regain his strikeout pitch as he led the American League in Ks with 245. Only two other pitchers on the staff, Mike Moore and Mike Morgan, won more than 10 games.

The situation at the plate was not much rosier. The Mariners placed 10th in the league in hitting with a .253 average and they were shut out more

times than anyone. They did have one moment in the sun, but unfortunately they were watching the blazing fastball of Roger Clemens strike out a major-league record 20 Mariners early in the campaign.

Jim Presley continued to show he is the third baseman of the future by belting 27 homers, knocking in 107 runs and batting .265. Presley had plenty of help from a terrific rookie, Danny Tartabull. Tartabull clouted 25 home runs, drove in 96 runs and batted .270. In a normal rookie year, Tartabull would have easily won the rookie of the year award, but instead, he didn't even finish in the money and then he was traded in the off season.

But then again, his fortunes mirrored his team's. And while Tartabull figures to get better, the Mariners don't.

PITCHERS
★ AND ★
ROOKIES

ROGER CLEMENS

On April 29, 1986, a new legend was born. That was the day Roger Clemens officially became the greatest strikeout pitcher in baseball. His name will be linked forever with all-time pitching greats like Sandy Koufax, Bob Feller, Tom Seaver, Nolan Ryan, Steve Carlton and Dizzy Dean. That night last April, Roger Clemens did the unthinkable, mowing down out 20 Seattle Mariners to set the new major league strikeout record for a nine inning game.

The fact that Clemens struck out 20 was remarkable, but the way he did it was even more impressive. Power pitchers, especially •when they're young, are usually prone to wildness. A case in point is a youthful Nolan Ryan. But Clemens proved on that night that not only is he a great strikeout pitcher, but a great pitcher, period.

Clemens allowed only three hits and issued no walks. Consider also that Clemens did it in the American League, where a designated hitter bats for the usually weak hitting pitcher. That was the beauty of his performance. He didn't just get the ball and fire it into catcher Rich Gedman's glove. He worked the count, worked the batter. A high, tight fastball on a 1-2 pitch. A curve away. He was a master pitcher with a couple of master pitches.

"This wasn't a rear back and throw," said Boston broadcaster Bob Montgomery. "He threw some really nasty pitches on 1-2 and 0-2 counts. I mean, just pieces of the ball were on the corner on both his fastball and breaking ball."

Clemens blew away everybody that night, striking out each Mariner at least once, sending down Phil Bradley all four times. He faced 30 batters, 12 were struck out swinging. He tied the American League record for consecutive strikeouts with eight (the mark held previously by Ryan and former Twin Ron Davis). But this was only a prelude for Clemens in 1986. While he didn't come close to matching that strikeout total during the

season, Clemens was just as dominating in other ways.

He finished the campaign with a sparkling 24-4 mark after beginning the season 14-0. He won the All-Star game, pitching three perfect innings and earning the Most Valuable Player award. His earned run average, 2.48, was tops in the American League and by unanimous vote he won the A.L. Cy Young award. To finish off the dream year, Clemens was voted the A.L.'s Most Valuable Player.

"To watch him is a pleasure," says Boston pitcher Bruce Hurst, "just for the other pitchers."

It is ironic that Clemens enjoyed such as dream season instead of a nightmarish one. Only eight months prior to the season, he underwent surgery on his forearm and a lingering question remained about the health of his arm. But there was never any doubt that, if healthy, Clemens would be an outstanding pitcher. That's not a judgment, that's a fact based on history.

Clemens starred for the University of Texas baseball team that won the College World Series in 1982. He was drafted in the first round, the 19th player selected in the 1983 June free agent pool, and quickly impressed the Boston organization. He began at Winter Haven in the Florida State League, won three of four decisions and yielded only 1.24 runs per nine innings before he was moved to New Britain of the Eastern League.

"He thought he should start in Double A," said Red Sox farm director Ed Kenney about Clemens and his confidence. "We thought he should start in A ball. I think it's better if a kid starts there and gets promoted rather than the reverse."

Going in reverse was the last thing Clemens had in mind. New Britain was a different league with similar results. Clemens won four of five decisions, had an e.r.a. of 1.38 and struck out 59 batters in 52 innings. In 1984, the Red Sox started him at their Triple A team in Pawtucket, but he handled International League hitters just the same. Earned run average? 1.93. Strikeouts? Fifty in 46.2 innings. From there, the only place was the major leagues and Clemens showed them a glimpse of his talent.

"I haven't seen anyone at the same stage who's got what he's got," said New Britain manager Ray Slider at

the time. "If he hadn't pitched as many innings as he's pitched this year, I'd say he could pitch in the big leagues right now."

"The most successful pitcher I ever had was Burt Hooton," said University of Texas coach Cliff Gustafson. "But he (Clemens) may be a better pro prospect. His control is amazing."

In his first 21 starts in the majors, Clemens posted a 9-4 record with a bloated 4.32 e.r.a. He did strike out a bunch of batters (126 in 133.1 innings) and it seemed only a matter of time before he began dominating at the top level. "His potential is almost unlimited," said Kenney.

Clemens went through a major set-back in 1985 with the Red Sox. He started strongly, but injured his pitching arm in July. He went on the disabled list, came back, then injured his arm again and was through for the season. His final totals were a 7-5 record with a 3.29 e.r.a. Solid numbers, but Clemens needed to undergo arm surgery, leaving some doubt as to whether he would be able to perform his best in 1986.

But that question was answered the night of April 29. The night Clemens became a legend.

DAVE RIGHETTI

Dave Righetti was relaxing in the clubhouse, all smiles, and clutching a bottle of champagne. It was the last day of the season and the Yankees took a doubleheader victory over the division-winning Red Sox. But that is not the reason why Righetti was so happy. The southpaw reliever saved both ends of the twinbill to set the major league record for saves by a relief pitcher with 46.

Though the Yankees were preparing to go home for the winter, the day was not forgotten by teammates. Not only was Righetti drinking the champagne, mostly he was wearing it. Righetti came on to save the first game by tossing one and two thirds innings of relief to tie Bruce Sutter's record of 45. Then in the nightcap, Righetti relieved former mate Brian Fisher (although Fisher didn't need any help) and retired Dave Sax for the final out. Boston fans booed, but manager Lou Piniella

---

Mike Scott (inset previous page), Dave Righetti (main picture) and Roger Clemens (facing page) were the pitching stars of '86.

Asheville of the Western Carolina League and posted a 3.14 e.r.a. He moved to Tulsa of the Texas League the following season and again pitched admirably. He caught the eye of the Yankees and New York demanded Righetti when they sent relief star Sparky Lyle to the Rangers as part of a big package deal.

Righetti continued where he left off and finally reached the majors in 1981. He starred in his rookie year, registering an 8-4 record with a microscopic 2.06 e.r.a. Righetti was named American League rookie of the year and he seemed·destined to be one of the greats.

But in 1982, Righetti had his problems. He started slowly and seemed to lose his control. It got so bad at one point that management sent him back to Columbus for more seasoning. After a short stint in Triple A he was back with the big club, but his stats were anything but

Dave Righetti (left, below and facing page) broke the American League record for saves with 46.

didn't care. He felt the man they call "Rags" deserved the record.

"He's been tremendous all year," said Piniella. "He's pitched in quite a few games where he didn't get the save and we won. He deserved it."

"I didn't care at all," Righetti said about breaking the record that way. "There's been too much heartache this year. I'm going to enjoy it. It's been just a great day for me. I'll have it for at least a year, until somebody else does it."

Righetti's entire season was great, not just the final day. The 28-year-old lefty finished the year 8-8 with a sparkling 2.45 earned run average. He appeared in 74 games, hurled 106.2 innings and, in a season of horrible pitching by the Yankees, was one of the lone bright spots.

The fact that Righetti had the chance to set the major league save record is more than ironic. For he began his career as a starter and with the Texas Rangers, not the Yanks.

Selected as the ninth player overall in the first round in 1977, the 6-3, 195 pound Righetti rose quickly through the Texas organization. In his first year, he won 11 of 14 decisions at

There was no letup in his performance, even though he viewed it as a step down.

"As a starter, there's more glamour," Righetti said. "You can see your name in the paper in the pitching line. You're more marketable for commercials and things, which I'd like to do. I thought I lost the chance for that two years ago, but now I feel I can help get that stuff for relievers."

If he keeps saving 46 games like he did in 1986, Rags will be starring in more than commercials.

MIKE SCOTT

The way most people in baseball talk, Mike Scott's picture should be on the wall of every post office in America. How else can a journeyman pitcher, who just three years ago sported a 5-11 record with a 4.68 earned run average, become the best pitcher in baseball at the age of 30? Nobody has ever heard of a 30-year-old phenom, have they? The only way that Scott could continue to get hitters out at the alarming rate he does is by cheating, right?

Well, there's more to the National League Cy Young award winner than just his 18-10 record, league leading 2.22 e.r.a and major league leading 306 strikeouts. Scott's got some solid history. Some interesting history.

Drafted by the Mets in the second round in 1976, Scott started to climb the ladder in the New York organization, starting at Jackson of the Texas League. After two seasons at Jackson, where he led the league in wins and innings pitched (his last year), the Mets promoted Scott to their Triple A affiliate in Tidewater. He pitched three more seasons in Tidewater before the Mets felt he was ready for the big leagues.

When he did arrive at Shea Stadium, it was only for a short stint as he was shuttled back and forth from the big leagues until he was in the majors to stay in 1981. His first two full seasons in New York brought him a very minor-league-like record of 12-23 with an e.r.a of well over 4.00.

The Mets tired waiting for him and they shipped him to the Astros for outfielder Danny Heep, strictly a minor deal. And after two sub-par years in Houston, Scott was looking more and more like he should find another occupation. His 90 mile-per–hour

impressive. He finished with an 11-10 record with a 3.79 e.r.a. The glaring problem on his pitching line was his walks to inning pitched ratio, as he yielded 108 free passes (the most in the majors) in 183 innings.

"Hitters made adjustments on me after my rookie year," Righetti said. "Mainly, they laid off and made me throw my breaking ball for strikes and I had some troubles early throwing strikes. Over the second half of the season, my control improved considerably. I'm always going to walk people. I could have taken care of the walks if I'd let up and throw the ball down the middle of the plate, but that isn't what got me to the big leagues or what'll get me where I want to be. It's a matter of learning and experience"

Obviously Righetti learned a lot that season, because in 1983 he was back to the overpowering Righetti that

the baseball world saw as a rookie. He peaked in a July 4 no-hit performance of the Boston Red Sox and finished the year 14-8. Then Yankee relief ace Goose Gossage took the free agent route to San Diego and George Steinbrenner ordered Righetti to take over as the bullpen ace starting in 1984.

"George really wanted me in the bullpen because he was deathly afraid he'd take the heat after Goose left," said Righetti, honestly. "Goose wanted to stick it to George, leave him in a bad situation. So George used me to take the heat off himself. He didn't mind putting the heat on me, just as long as he wasn't embarrassed."

Righetti stood the heat well, earning 31 saves his first season in a relief role. A year later, Rags saved 29 games, won 12 and pitched to the tune of 2.78 earned run average.

Mike Scott (above, right and facing page) frustrated hitters all season with his split-fingered fastball. He led the major leagues in strikeouts and won the N.L. Cy Young award.

fastball was being tattooed by big league hitters.

"There was no guessing," Scott says. "Well, they were guessing, but they'd guess fastball and they'd get one. If you get behind 2-1 or 3-1 and they know the fastball is coming, even if you throw it 95 miles an hour, they're gonna hit it harder than you throw it."

Then he struck gold. A month before spring training in 1985, former Astros general manager Al Rosen suggested that Scott go to San Diego to get tutoring from Roger Craig, the master of the split-fingered fastball, who had just retired. Scott agreed, saying, "I couldn't go out there throwing the same thing I did in '84. My slider was no good in '84. I messed around with a curveball I've always thrown, but that's never been very good."

Ten days later Scott had a new pitch in his repertoire, a split-fingered fastball that dips at the last moment, giving the illusion that it's a spitter.

"I didn't have much control with it at first," Scott admits. "I was throwing balls that bounced. But guys were swinging. Right away, people were

swinging at pitches that were bouncing in the dirt. I've never been a strikeout pitcher but all of a sudden I'm getting ahead of the hitters with the split-finger, setting them up and striking them out with the fastball."

Not only did Scott start striking them out, he just plain started getting them out. In 1985, Scott registered an 18-8 mark with a 3.29 e.r.a., far and away his finest season in the major leagues. He also struck out 137 batters, his best mark and the only time in his career he got into triple figures in Ks.

His success continued last year, but with more startling results. All of a sudden Scott was the toughest pitcher in the league, striking out batters like he was Nolan Ryan and being generally unhittable. In fact he was literally unhittable on the day the Astros clinched the pennant, tossing a no-hitter against the Giants and striking out 13 in the process.

The only problem with his success was that it was so sudden, everybody accused him of cheating. There was no way his pitch could dive so much without the help of a foreign substance. Sandpaper was the method most players and managers suspected. And earlier this year, an opposing manager asked the umpires to check the ball three times in one inning. The manager? Roger Craig.

"That's O.K. by me," Scott says. "If they're worried about that stuff, it's an advantage for me."

"As much as I admire and respect Mike Scott, I think he's doing something to scuff the ball," Craig said after one game. "We found evidence of the ball being scuffed and showed it to the umpires, but it was between innings and he said we had to catch him in the act, between pitches. A lot of guys like to use sandpaper. They glue it to their glove hand."

The cheating accusations came to a head in the playoffs as Scott easily handled the Mets for the two Houston wins. The Mets even kept a box of baseballs they said Scott scuffed.

"Every single ball was scuffed. Every one of them," said Mets second baseman Wally Backman following Scott's second victory. "You know there are people in the game who cheat. I never knew until late in the game, but when you have 15 to 20 balls that have been scuffed, you know it's not done by fouling them off. I don't know how he was doing it. I assume it's something in his glove hand."

But unless the Mets or anybody else can prove Mike Scott cheats, the man is innocent until proven guilty. After all this is America, the land of freedom and opportunity. Just ask Mike Scott: he took the opportunity to learn the split-fingered fastball and become one of the best pitchers in baseball.

★★★

ROOKIES

WALLY JOYNER

The sign in right field at Anaheim Stadium is there almost every game. It says "Wallyworld," and for most of last season, Wally Joyner of the California Angels seemed to be in his own little world. Pitches down and away, Joyner defensively lifted to leftfield for a single. Pitches that were down the middle were sent right back through the middle. And pitches that were inside, Joyner pulled to the deepest parts of right field. There's no doubt that "Wallyworld" was a fun place to be in 1986.

"I don't consider myself a phenom or anything," Joyner says nonchalantly. "There will be rough times. I'm just enjoying this."

Not many of the pitchers enjoyed being in "Wallyworld", as Joyner finished the season batting .290 with 22 home runs and 100 RBI. Rough times for Joyner? Hah, say most of the baseball people around him.

"I expected him to be a good player, but I didn't expect this at all," says Angels manager Gene Mauch. "If he had hit 15 home runs all year, that wouldn't have been bad. I guess somebody's had this kind of start as a rookie before, but I can't think who it might be."

"We thought he'd be a Rusty Staub," says California general manager Mike Port. "A high-average hitter with occasional power. The home runs are a surprise but, hey, we'll take 'em."

Before his first season in the big leagues, Joyner never hit more than 12 round-trippers in one campaign. But it wasn't only his home run power that catapulted him to fame. The fact that Joyner was replacing the greatest hitter of his time, Rod Carew, helped bring him to the forefront.

At age 24, California management felt Joyner was ready, so Carew was released during the offseason. And when spring training began, there were no less than five veteran first basemen in line for the job Joyner won. Of course there was pressure, but it was Joyner who applied even more of it on himself.

"He put burdens on himself and tried to live up to them," says former MVP, now broadcaster, Joe Torre. "He's repeatedly said he's under pressure to replace Carew. Nobody here wants him to do anything like that. But it's something he's living up to."

One area where he has far surpassed Carew is in endorsements. As "Wallyworld" started heating up, his agent began sifting through literally hundreds of offers for his services such as:
- Wally Bars
- WallyVision
- Air Joyner Footwear
- A Wally Doll
- A Wally Workout Tape
- The Wally Joyner Story (in paperback or hardcover)

"Our company has represented a lot of big names – Greg Luzinski, Larry Bowa and Jerry Reuss – but none has ever exploded like Wally has," says Joyner's agent, Steve Freyer, of the Sports Advisors Group. "Wally has met up with every kind of shyster in the world and Wally, being the nice guy that he is, sits down and listens to them. Now he finally tells them, 'Look, it sounds great, but why don't you call my agent?'"

There's no question that Joyner's popularity reached Fernandomania-type proportions in 1986. He garnered 980,000 votes in the the All-Star balloting to overtake the Yankees' Most Valuable Player Don Mattingly for the American League first base starting assignment. But those aren't the only fans he made.

"Joyner scares the hell out of me," says Baltimore Orioles scout Jim Russo. "He's something special. He's one of the best I've seen come up in a long time.

"The first thing you say to yourself is, 'Pitch him away. But I'll be darned if you can do that because he can hit it out to left, too. High changeup? No. High fastball? No. A breaking ball away? No... He's handled everything."

"He's the most impressive rookie I've ever seen," said teammate Reggie Jackson, a pretty fair player in his prime. "He handles himself as if he'd been in this league for years. There's nothing more you could want out of a kid."

Joyner has always been a player that can hit for average. In three minor league seasons before joining the big leagues, Wally hit .328, .317 and .283. His shortcoming was power and he knew that to play first base at the major league level, he would need to get a little more punch in his bat.

"I was a skinny kid with a big butt," he recalls. "That's why the scouts may not have liked me. My baseball coach at Brigham Young took me sight unseen and was a little disappointed when he saw I was six feet tall and 160 pounds. I tried weights once, but my body never accepted them."

He tried again two seasons ago and his body accepted them graciously. He went to Mayaguez of the Puerto Rican Winter League and ripped the pitchers, hitting .356 with 14 homers and 48 RBI, and winning the Triple Crown for the first time in that circuit in 24 years. His tremendous winter play gave the Angels a glimpse of what they could expect. "What he did in Puerto Rico is only indicative of what he can do," said Mauch prior to spring training. "It doesn't mean he'll do it in the big leagues, but it's an indication that he has the ability."

Not only does Joyner have the ability, but he put it on display for everyone to see in 1986. As the sign in rightfield says, "It's a Wallyworld."

PETE INCAVIGLIA

The legend of Pete Incaviglia started on the major league level on the first day of batting practice at the Texas Rangers' spring training camp. With the sun shining and teammates watching, Incaviglia blistered hit after hit until he cracked the big one. With one mighty swing, Incaviglia squashed a line drive that actually splintered a hole in the outfield fence at Municipal Stadium in Pompano Beach, Florida.

The true legend of Pete Incaviglia really began at Oklahoma State, where he belted 48 home runs, drove in 143 runs in 75 games, and even hit .464 in his junior season. In his three seasons at Oklahoma State, Incaviglia crushed 100 home runs with a batting average of .398. He was selected by the Montreal Expos in the 1985 June draft, but he refused to sign, forcing Montreal to ship him to Texas, where he gladly signed a $175,000 signing bonus.

At 6-3, 225 pounds, Incaviglia looks like he can hit a baseball, but until that day in spring training, scouts around the league were skeptical. After all, the only bat Incaviglia used in college was aluminum, a bat that's illegal in the major leagues. Many felt that his production would fall dramatically if he were to use the standard wood bat. But those close to him knew differently.

"The day I met Pete's brother, Tony, here last winter, I saw him walk over to the dugout, so I went over to shake hands," says Texas manager Bobby Valentine. "He was staring up at the billboard out there (an airplane about 550 feet from home plate was on it) and he looked at me and said, 'Pete's going to hit one off that plane someday.' Can you believe that?"

Incaviglia hit his seventh home run of spring training on the last day, breaking the Rangers' spring record held by Jeff Burroughs in 1974. With Incaviglia swinging a hot bat, Texas faithful were hoping he wasn't a second coming of David Clyde or even Dave Hostetler.

"It's hard to compare an everyday player to an 18-year-old pitcher who was fresh out of high school and shouldn't have been there in the first place," said Rangers GM Tom Grieve, comparing Incaviglia to Clyde. "Incaviglia made this team because of his talent. David Clyde made this team because of his appeal.

"Hoss (Hostetler) created a lot of excitement when he hit all those home runs (11 in his first 91 at bats) during one stretch there in 1982. He was written up big in the papers and people were calling the talk shows to ask about him. In that sense, he and Pete are similar. But talent-wise, there's no comparison. Incaviglia has a better swing, better makeup, better speed, is a better defensive player and is five or six years younger than Hoss was."

For the brash and confident Incaviglia, there were some tentative times. "I had the tiniest bit of doubt this spring," he admitted. "I had some questions because I didn't know what to expect. I just went out and worked hard every day and kept telling myself, 'Have a good spring and you'll be there.' Now here I am."

And how. Incaviglia exploded onto the major league scene by belting 30 home runs, driving in 88 runs and hitting .250. He added 21 doubles and had the game-winning RBI 11

times. Not bad for someone the scouts weren't sure of.

"I can play this game," Incaviglia says. "I can play here and help this team win. As long as I'm relaxed at the plate and seeing the ball well, I'm going to hit a lot of home runs.

It's a great, great feeling. There's nothing like it. You're down two runs in the seventh and you step up and hit a three-run homer – that's tops. It's a reward for all the hard work."

"He's unique," says Valentine. "I have a hard time comparing him to anyone. All I know is that when Ted Williams calls Zig (trainer Bill Zeigler), he keeps asking about him.

"He's aggressive with a ton of self-confidence. If I had that ability, I'd be aggressive and self-confident, too. Pete's fun-loving. He's competitive and he's daring. He's the type of guy in a poker game who would bump the pot trying to hide an inside straight."

The kind of guy legends are made of.

JOSE CANSECO

No rookie last year had to live up to more expectations than Jose Canseco. The Oakland A's young star leaped through the farm system with startling numbers, then gave a glimpse of things to come with a short September call-up in 1985 that nobody can forget.

There was Jose, crouched forward, open to the pitching rubber. His left foot is planted almost on the edge of the batter's box. As the pitch heads home, Canseco straightens and recoils like a snake ready to attack. And that's exactly what American League pitchers felt like – snake-bit.

In his short stint in September, Canseco blasted five tremendous home runs, knocked in 13 runs and hit .302 in 29 games. It was almost as impressive as his trek through the system. He began the year in the A's Huntsville, Alabama team (Southern League) and hit 25 homers, drove in 80 runs and hit .318 in only 58 games due to a fractured finger.

He quickly leaped from Double A ball to the A's Triple A team in Tacoma. There, Canseco hit .348 with 11 homers and 47 RBI in 60 games. Add in the final month of the season with the A's, and his cumulative stats for the year read 147 games, 41 home runs, 140 RBI and a .328 batting

average. Not bad for a kid that was picked in the 15th round, a kid that stood 6-3 but weighed only 170 pounds. Now, after adding about 50 pounds of muscle, Canseco was ready to show the world what he could do.

"The trick to me is how he could handle the attention, all the distractions of being a major league player," said Oakland director of player development Karl Kuehl during spring training. "He has been very good in local theaters and now he's going to Carnegie Hall. But I think he'll handle it all. He is going to put some big numbers on the board."

Kuehl proved quite prophetic. Canseco finished second in the American League in RBI with 117, and fourth in home runs with 33. A late season slump brought his average down to .240, but couldn't dampen the enthusiasm about his talent and future.

"He hits the ball as hard as anyone in the game," said Oakland hitting instructor Bob Watson. "The thing that he has is bat speed. He might not hit the ball on the screws, but he still hits it to all fields.

"Jose can miss a ball, like (Mickey) Mantle did, and hit it out of the park, especially to the opposite field. The average hitter has to get everything going for him to hit it out of the park.

"He's so damn strong. You know what I worry about? I'm afraid he's going to hit the ball so hard up the middle one day that he's going to kill the pitcher."

"Lord, he has a wicked cut," said Boston's flamboyant pitcher Oil Can Boyd. "I once gave him my best, the screwball, and he went after it. He hit it as high as he did hard."

Canseco's pro career has been fairly steady in performance except for 1984, when his mother died. Canseco took the loss hard, but rebounded nicely for Modesta of the California League.

"He has matured, both mentally and physically," said his former Tacoma manager Keith Lieppman. "He has taken control of himself. He has had a number of setbacks along the way, such as the death of his mother, with whom he was very close. But he has used them as building blocks. He has grown up a lot faster than most people I've seen between 17 and 21. He has got great raw talent,

but he has improved as much inside as outside."

"It's been a combination of things," says Canseco about his development. "Maturing, getting older and my weight training."

Said former Oakland manager Jackie Moore, "We're talking about a kid with exceptional ability. I don't know how good he can get."

The rest of the American League is just finding out.

WILL CLARK

Unlike most of the highly-publicized rookies that made a big splash in the major leagues in 1986, Will Clark of the San Francisco Giants is not a power hitter. Sure he'll pop a round-tripper on occasion, but contrary to the likes of Jose Canseco, Pete Incaviglia and Wally Joyner, Clark is more of a quintessential hitter.

The lefty swinging Clark is more apt to spray the ball around, a line drive to left field, a bloop to center or a hard liner inside the first base bag. He can be compared more favorably to a

It was a wonderful season for rookies and none were better than Oakland's Jose Canseco (above left). The righthanded power hitter belted 33 homers in capturing the rookie award. Pete Incaviglia (above right) smacked 30 dingers for Texas.

Keith Hernandez than a Canseco. But what Canseco and the rest can supply in power, Clark replaces with an uncanny knack for the dramatic that's followed him throughout his career.

In his first major league at-bat against the Astros in Houston, Clark joined 52 others in the record books when he crushed a Nolan Ryan pitch over the centerfield fence for a home run. This after Ryan gave him some chin music on a 1-2 count.

In his professional debut for the Giants' farm team in Fresno, Clark belted a home run in his initial at-bat and then added another one later in the contest. In the Giants' first exhibition game of the spring, again Clark homered.

"Will Clark is the type of player that comes along only now and then," said San Francisco general manager Al Rosen. "Some guys are born to play. Will is a natural."

"Will had 'Major Leaguer' written all over him from the day he reported to spring training," said Giants manager Roger Craig. "We knew from the start that he had the physical tools and we found out he could handle it mentally."

While Clark's rookie campaign was more than successful, it was dotted with injuries. Twice Clark was out for extended period and each time he ended up on the disabled list. Clark did finish the season hitting .287 with 11 home runs, 47 runs batted in, 27 doubles and 8 game-winning RBI. But even that production was unexpected considering the amount of time he spent in the minors.

Clark reached the major league level faster than any Giants regular player since World War II. Prior to Clark, a guy by the name of Willie Mays held the Giants' record by appearing in only 116 games in the minors before reaching the big time. Clark's rise

through baseball, however, is filled with more of the dramatic.

Drafted by the Kansas City Royals in 1982, Clark rejected their bid and decided to play college ball at Mississippi State instead. As a freshman, Clark replaced the starting first baseman who was injured (his name wasn't Wally Pipp), and promptly got six hits in eight trips in a doubleheader against Louisiana State. His next game, against Alabama, Clark swatted two homers and a double. His success never stopped after that. By his sophomore campaign, Clark earned All-America honors by batting .438 with 25 homers and 83 RBI. He was chosen to play for the United States Olympic baseball team and responded by batting .397 with 16 homers and 43 RBI. In five Olympic games, Clark hit .429 with eight runs batted in on three round-trippers.

Clark enjoyed continued success

at Mississippi State and the Giants selected him second overall in the June 1984 draft.

"As a pure hitter, Clark is as good as they come," said Clark's Olympic coach Rod Dedeaux. "He's relaxed at the plate. He has a quick bat, makes good contact and hits to all fields."

After being drafted, Clark signed and immediately went to Fresno where he batted .309 with 10 homers and 48 RBI. Following the season, he went to the Arizona instructional League and tore the cover off the ball, hitting .487. Despite his impressive statistics, the Giants were virtually convinced that Clark would start the season in the minors, not wanting to rush a top prospect before he was ready. Clark took care of that in spring training, by hitting .297 and fielding his position with ease.

"I was thinking about making this club from the start," Clark said after making the team. "I wasn't worried

The Giants' Will Clark shows his versatility by being able to use his sweet stroke for power (above) or for just laying down a bunt. The rookie batted .284 in his first season. Don Naylor (overleaf) proved to be a vital acquistion for the Red Sox as he led them to a World Series berth.

about it because I had no say in the matter. I came to camp with a lot of confidence, so I was relaxed.

"I wanted to make the club, but I had no timetable for reaching the big leagues. Roger (Craig) told me if I was ready, I'd play every day. I had no problem with that. All I can say is that I'm very proud to be the first baseman of the Giants."

You can be sure the Giants are just as proud having him. And even if he doesn't possess the power of Canseco, Incaviglia or Joyner, Clark does have something they don't possess. The flair for the dramatic.